I hope you find this small book helpful as a guide in STEALING HOME. Rosedog Press has produced a handsome handbook...with one exception. The usual materials found toward the front of the book, prior to the actual text, have been placed in the rear of the book, at the conclusion of the text. So, in order to find items such as The Table of Contents, Dedication, Acknowledgment, Introduction, and further information About the Book and About the Author, you should turn to the rear of the book, where, starting on page 83, you will find these items. Hopefully, this detour will not interfere with your orderly reading of this material.

Sebastian MacDonald

Stealing Home

by

Sebastian K. MacDonald, C.P.

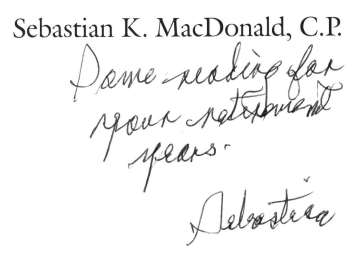

RoseDog ❀ Books

PITTSBURGH, PENNSYLVANIA 15222

RoseDog Books
701 Smithfield Street
Pittsburgh, PA 15222
Visit our website at *www.rosedogbookstore.com*

ISBN: 978-1-4349-3183-2
eISBN: 978-1-4349-2493-3

Chapter 1

Perspectives

A perspective is an outlook on life, a point of view. Everyone is endowed with a perspective. In fact, most of us are likely equipped with several perspectives, if not simultaneously, then probably sequentially. They are the windows out of which we look at our surroundings. But, in that function, they also provide an inward looking glance, that gives us access to our inner selves, and the way we work.

We're born with a proclivity toward a perspective. It is innate. To some extent, it modifies the time-honored recognition that we are born *tabula rasa*-like, that is, empty and devoid of any preconceptions. This seems true, even while we recognize that we will, sooner rather than later, begin to express ourselves out of a definite point of view. No particular perspective is necessarily indelible. We probably tinker with our perspective(s) once we become aware of their operation within us. However, it's possible that we never become aware of them. We may go through life with a distinctive viewpoint on events, situations and persons, without ever questioning how, or why, we see our surroundings the way we do. There's no particular problem with this, unless our outlook on life emerges out of kilter, if not in our own estimation, then in that of others, who might call our attention to what they consider a strange point of view on a number of matters. At that juncture, we might pause and reflect that there is some merit to this observation.

A perspective has an element of uniqueness about it, corresponding closely to the kind of person I am. The notion of uniqueness, of course, admits of degrees. In reality, few of us are so unique that we stand off completely different from others. If that were the case, it would be difficult to share, communicate or collaborate with them. Apart from rather rare instances, the uniqueness of a perspective is, at best, partial. Factually, in most cases we share perspectives with others, and this establishes a social dimension to perspective, to a degree.

A perspective is an asset. It's our window on the world. Without it, we would, in some measure, be cut off from our surroundings, out of touch with them. But we seldom experience this situation. It's more accurate to reflect that, without a perspective, we would be too perplexed by what we daily encounter to cope with it all. There's simply too much out there seeking to engage our attention, even demanding that we heed and attend to it, and challenging our ability to handle it. Happily, perspective comes to our rescue as an angle of vision on what lies before us, enabling us to engage these surroundings, admittedly, in a limited way. All of this illustrates why perspective is a window through which we look and see our surroundings. It facilitates our awareness, though in a limited and curtailed way. Indeed, borrowing from George Lakoff the term "framing", helps us to describe what perspective does for one: it frames a portion of the world before us, enabling an individual to gaze at and recognize it.[1]

So, at one and the same time, we acknowledge that perspective gives us access to truth and reality, but, not to all truth or to the entirety of reality—a prerogative of God alone. (For this reason, the suggestion is made, in what follows, that our view on what lies beyond us may not always be correct). We are not made to handle all truth or all reality in one fell swoop, but we must approach it gradually, over time, little by little. So, at one and the same time, perspective gives entrée to what is around us so that we are aware and in touch with it, while, at the same time, protecting us from being completely overrun by more than we can engage or negotiate.

A perspective is comparable to a window in a house. We can stand before the window and look out through it at the street in front of the house, noting the activity occurring on it. We do see the street. We need

---

[1] Matt Bai, "The Framing Wars," *New York Times Magazine*, 17 July 2005.

not worry that what we see is a chimera. However, we realize that the street is longer than the portion we see through the window, and that there are sights to be seen on either side of the window frame, that escape us, leaving us unaware of them. This obviously limits our access to the reality nearby us. But normally we have little reason to complain about this, having a minimal or no sense of being deprived of something we want to see. For the most part, we're satisfied with what we presently see through our living room window. It allows access to see enough of what meets our needs or desires at the moment.

But it may be that we're dissatisfied with our living room window, precisely because it is too small or narrow, curtailing our vision more than we prefer. We may wish to augment what we can observe. If such is the case, we can enlarge the window, calling in a carpenter to expand the framework encompassing the window. At the end of this project, we will indeed see more, but, despite this improvement, we will still be unable to see everything out there. We will see more of it, but not all of it.

We can transpose this example to our own composition, and the way we are made. For, we operate in dependence on perspectives, from the very beginning of our existence. And they're likely to be with us throughout our lives, in some form or fashion. We can remain satisfied with the outlook on life that they provide us. Or, it can gradually dawn upon us, in one way or another, that they're inadequate, and are not serving us as well or as fully as we should desire. If this be so, we can change, or at least adjust, our perspective(s) on things. We might do this by associating with people who see things differently than we do, by listening to their points of view, and by allowing ourselves to be influenced by them. This will constitute a reeducation of ourselves.

We can do much the same through reading or accessing other media of information. We can come to see that there's more than one way to view a topic or issue about which we have had our own point of view. This may lead us to judge the viewpoint out of which we customarily operate to need enlargement or adjustment. In fact, this process may be called for throughout life. This will frequently be in response to various experiences that we undergo in the course of our life (more about this will be addressed in chapter three of this book). However, it is unlikely that we will ever completely disabuse ourselves of those early, innate, outlooks on life that seemed to coincide with our genetic packaging.

They tend to be so deeply engrained in us that, though possibly adjustable in some measure to influences that we undergo, they are unlikely to be thoroughly and totally set aside for ever.

Perspectives are indeed subject to the many influences we undergo from our life experiences. Not each and every adjustment we make in response is for the better. While some of the early outlooks on our ambience may need improvement, this need not involve all of them, as if the original composition of our individuality was defective. It may have been in need of improvement, but this doesn't imply significant distortions in how we look out upon our surroundings. After all, should we evaluate the basic frame of reference guiding us, on a scale of one to ten, we can rightly regard anything beyond a one as an asset to be valued. But this doesn't mean that the role played by a basic point of view, scoring at the low end of this scale, is as helpful as what it might be if it was operative at the higher end.

We should note that, among the influences bearing upon the perspective(s) by we engage our surroundings, are those from God Himself. In fact, in the last analysis, everything we're attributing here to our initial human composite is traceable to the finger of God, as our Creator. Indeed, in keeping with this conviction about the divine influence on our origins and early existence, we are positioned to acknowledge further examples of God operative in our life. We sometimes refer to these in terms describing God's Providence in our regard. We believe in His providential oversight of ourselves as pervasive and all-encompassing, much more than we can comprehend and appreciate. As believers, we ascribe a universal oversight to God regarding both our composition and our agency—by and large beyond any appreciative awareness on our part. This extends to God's role in the fundamental perspectives that are a prominent instance of His provision for us. Whether we choose to designate it by the name of a common or generic grace, made available to all God's children in this world, and present prior to subsequent forms of grace with which He will endow at least some of us, with the passage of time, or whether we prefer to acknowledge this gift of His as part of His overall providence, we acknowledge that we can't adequately appreciate the genesis and workings of perspective in our life, without acknowledging God's part in it.

At this juncture, there is room to surmise what some longstanding perspectives within us might be. At the risk of becoming embroiled in examples of overused labeling, we might readily admit that the familiar descriptions "conservative" and "liberal" come to mind as readily observable points of view characteristic of most of us. We understand the conservative viewpoint as slow to accept a position until it is firmly established, and as reluctant to set aside what has worked well in the past, while willing to move ahead slowly so long as the passageway seems secure. In its turn, we regard the liberal viewpoint as ready to investigate a position recently advanced, because sensitive to problems with some past practices that prevail in the present, and as prone to experiment with other promising formulae or programs.

These are ways of looking out on out life settings that often accompany us from the beginning. At the outset, it is unlikely that we have pursued them on our own initiative, or tried to learn about them from other sources. They have simply constituted part of our makeup. However, these frames of reference are not cast in stone. They can undergo change. We perhaps know of people moving from one point of view to another. So our viewpoints can change. Every child is born into a family where it is influenced by the latter's way of doing things, and its outlooks on a variety of situations. Often, as the young person matures, the points of view absorbed from the family are still evident in his or her life. But, quite frequently, the offspring follow their own perspectives, which may differ markedly from their parents', even while yet manifesting strains of its influence.

Closely paralleling this example is another, that is age related. We sometimes note that an older person tends to be conservative, on the basis of a lifetime of experience that has served him or her well, while a younger individual, relying on a pent-up store of energy and enterprise, tends to be liberal minded, regarding him or herself equal to new and unexpected challenges. But, to repeat, these classifications too facilely become stereotypes.

There are also significant interconnections between perspective and other components of our behavior, which will be addressed in chapters to come, such as inclinations, vocation, freedom, experience, culture, suffering, sin, etc. But amid them all, an important influence to factor in is our religious faith, given its role in shaping our outlook on God's presence in our life, especially through scripture and tradition, as conveyed by the church.

Faith too plays itself out in various, sometimes divergent, ways among those who share it, and this can also emerge in the perspectives whereby we affirm His operations upon and around us. A perennial example concerns His role in the origins of both world and universe. While all people of faith profess belief in God's involvement in this process, some do so from a point of view that attributes every detail of life's beginnings, whether it be human, animal, organic, mineral, aquatic, geologic, or planetary, to God's intimate involvement with it, while other believers frame God's activity in creation in an evolutionary mode, which, while accompanying His creative design down through the ages, does so by way of the inherent powers and energies He has embedded in the created order.

Faith also commends to us an important role for the church, which, again, can be approached from different angles. While Catholics entertain a profound reverence for the church, in both its teachings and its practices, once again, they do so off of different angles of vision. For instance, with the passage of time, the church may see fit to modify some of her positions. This may be acceptable to some of her adherents, but it can occasion misgivings for others of her membership. In each instance, there are variants in viewpoints on something like cultic worship. Though these are hardly innate, they have often been imbued in people at an early age, by respected teachers and clergy. In the aftermath of Vatican II, for example, following its approval of changes in so vital a church activity as liturgy, the perspective of some of the faithful regarding worship has been challenged, and they find it difficult to negotiate the required adjustments in outlook.

It should be noted that, given the variety inherent in the perspectives whereby we look out on our world, (some of which have just been noted), it is quite likely some perspectives or outlooks will prove to be less helpful, while others will be more so, at least in some instances. Notwithstanding this, even an apparently erroneous viewpoint on situations doesn't necessarily make a person dysfunctional or inoperative. One can manage one's life fairly adequately, despite being misguided by a distorted perspective that affects an assessment of the surroundings around us. While a misconception can prove bothersome, to say the least, it doesn't necessarily prove disastrous. The human person can be adept at maneuvering, even if somewhat clumsily, despite the handicap of basic misconceptions about one's environment.

Nonetheless, it is a beneficial exercise to review the perspectives that so affect the way we engage the world about us. From the vantage point of moral theology, especially in its social guidance, it is quite helpful to appreciate where both we and others "are coming from". Since moral theology seeks to provide a sense of direction on how to conduct our lives, we need a proper orientation toward what is good and what is evil, so as to live as disciples of Christ, especially in an atmosphere whose values are set by others, whose point of view differs from ours. A conviction about what is good or evil (what is or is not imitative of Christ) is a fundamental concern for believers. It cannot be appreciated only in terms of behavior and conduct, since our agency is nearly always beholden to deeper sources, such as the frames of reference through which we see what lies around us. At times we must negotiate the differences in this area between ourselves and others, and it helps each of us to appreciate where the other is coming from. Often unnecessary conflict can be avoided by making this effort.

An appreciation of the role of perspective, in our life, as well as that of others, can illuminate why we, or they, act the way we do, or don't. Some of our activity, for instance, may disturb others, leading them to ascribe some kind of moral liability to what we do or say (or don't), when, as a matter of fact, we're acting out of a mindset to which we are oblivious, despite its apparent moral inappropriateness. On the other hand, the situation may prevail, where others tend to exonerate us because we are the way we are, in large part due to our way of looking at things—a way with which they are familiar, though perhaps they disagree with it. While this may not be complimentary to us, it does free us of unethical conduct, at least in their estimation. Familiarity with others' ways of looking at things, as frequently happens in marriage, can obviate conflicts despite the residue of different viewpoints remaining.

But, we do everyone a favor if we come to terms with the perspectives out of which we operate, reviewing them, and possibly adjusting what can and should be improved. While moral theology focuses primarily on deliberate behavior, it is also interested in discovering influences on conduct traceable to factors such as basic viewpoints, calling upon other disciplines to come into play, to explore and possibly discover and adjust them, if necessary.

But to the extent we operate out of frames of reference that we have consciously nurtured and developed, then moral theology can come into play, to address such situations. This can become a vigorous, strenuous process, that makes demands on us. This exercise can become ascetical in nature, that is, a kind of spiritual regimen of purging and readjusting the terms out of which we operate. Though this effort might reinvigorate the time-honored practice of an examination of conscience, it can also lead us past this into the wellsprings of who we are, where some possibly beneficial discoveries await us. As Jesus remarks: "When your eye is sound, then your whole body is filled with light…" (Lk 11.34). Perhaps that is why so many of His miracles consisted of restoring eyesight to the blind. Possibly what was at stake here was not only physical sight, but perspectives and viewpoints out of which a person looks at life to gain an accurate view of what lies ahead.

Chapter 2

Inclinations

Concern about the horizon enveloping the world we inhabit is a beneficial preoccupation. Looking out on life's landscape from a skewed perspective is, to say the least, unhelpful. It likely disadvantages us in making our way through life. So it is beneficial to be aware of our basic viewpoints.

This is only part of a task, however, that some versions of moral theology take upon themselves, in an effort to provide helpful guidelines on how to discover, and obtain, aids in doing the good and avoiding the evil. There is a concomitant project, closely connected with perspective, centering on other influential orientations within us: our inclinations and tendencies. These too deserve our attention, for they bear just as significantly upon our behavior, and ultimately on the type of person we are, or are becoming. It should not be surprising to discover the close symmetry between how we look out at life, and how we tend toward it, or react to it. It's a matter of the linkage between a way of acquiring awareness, and the drives or tendencies consequent upon it. It's quite unlikely that divergence would develop between them to the point where the way we perceive our situation in the world exerts little influence on the way we respond to it. Perhaps some instances of severe malfunctioning within us might result in such a discrepancy, but this is not to be presumed.

One basic distinction frequently associated with inclinations is that between those who are outwardly oriented, and others who are inwardly attracted. There is no reason to draw immediate conclusions about the moral significance of either movement in our lives. An outwardly tending person finds him or herself reaching beyond the self for satisfaction or fulfillment, whether that be in persons, activities or situations that lay beyond oneself. This doesn't necessarily imply any disenchantment with one's own self, as if it were deficient or incapable of achieving satisfactory goals. It merely indicates the spontaneous proclivity someone has to reach out as a satisfying way of expending one's energy to engage one's interests. But, in situations where such ventures are unavailable, a certain restlessness ensues should one be thrown back on his or her own resources. Being alone with oneself may not be a welcome prospect for someone who enjoys being with others, or circulating in different kinds of settings. He or she will be less likely to flourish as a human person, should an individual be curtailed to activity within an enclosed situation, with no outlets.

There is a corresponding perspective to this, fully aware of attractive opportunities opening out before a person in a situation, which, in turn, constitutes a strong enticement for exploration and engagement. An outwardly inclining person becomes energized at the dawning possibility of meeting someone or something beyond oneself, and thrives in settings where this happens. Such a one is described as an activist, or, perhaps, an extrovert. In the gospel, Martha, the sister of Lazarus and Mary, illustrates a person like this, with an outgoing tendency; she needed to be in contact with others in order to be herself (Jn 11 and 12).

On the other hand, there is another type of person who is comfortable being at home with oneself. This person is endowed with a perspective that finds much to engage his or her attention, close to home, even within the confines of one's own self. He or she enjoys a perspective that sees so much close at hand, even deep within oneself, that it provides a satisfying view of one's ambience, sufficient to enrich one's outlook on life and the opportunities available there. The frame of reference of this kind of person provides as much data and information as is needed, close at hand though it be, to satisfy one's curiosity and need to know. This kind of person presumably displays a set of tendencies or proclivities closely aligned with the viewpoint opening up before him or her. That is to say, such a person will lean the way one sees things, and, when the window frame through which one looks is largely focused on what is near at hand, then one's energies will be powered up precisely in those terms. Such a person will find much within oneself, or near at hand, to engage one's attention. He or she will naturally incline toward exploring within or nearby, finding enough there to meet one's needs. This type of individual might be regarded as an introvert, and comprises a group frequently consisting of artists, poets, musicians, academics, policy-makers, inventors, etc. Such a one flourishes in closing off oneself from distractions, so as to allow full engagement to take place with what is close at hand, to which one has a strong attraction. Again reverting to the gospels, we recall Mary, the sister of Martha (above), and identify her as a person perfectly content to explore what is at hand, in her own home, the world near at hand, to seek her development and fulfillment.

The area of truth telling illustrates how one's basic inclination expresses itself. When one finds support in the presence of others to express his or her interpretation of a situation, he or she may do so freely and confidently. This tendency, which is really a premoral one largely antecedent to any deliberate decision to be so oriented, is often quite conducive to truth telling, though it must be alert to telling too much to too many too enthusiastically. On the other hand, when one is more inclined to inward dialogue with oneself, or within an intimate circle of friends, the evident orientation here is to keep a lid on truth telling by telling too little to too few too cautiously. This, in its turn, can be quite beneficial in many of life's arenas, but it may falter in forthrightness. Each of these basic inclinations, faultless in their early stages of development, underlies full-blown moral activity, whether for weal or woe. There is a correspondence here between perspective and inclination, though this works itself out in less than precise ways. That is to say, someone who tends to be outspoken is not thereby automatically an extrovert, or another, inclined to keep an opinion to oneself, is not by that very fact an introvert.

Inclinations, however, even more so than perspectives, suggest moral implications. That is to say, they give indications, in their modes of operation, of how one might act when capable of full deliberation about a situation. For they are not early stages of mental operations, as viewpoints are, but are movement oriented energies, even though not yet full-blown engagements between a person whose capacities are completely developed, and one's surroundings. They're only inklings of this, mere suggestions of the way a person is inclined to act. But they do hint at what might bloom into full-scale conduct. Even at an early stage of maturation, they tell us something significant about ourselves as prospective, mature moral agents. These tendencies within us are both promising and threatening. They point us toward the good we might achieve with our lives. But they also suggest the evils looming before us.

Like perspective, inclination is innate. It is not something that emerges for the first time later in life, when we are more mature. It describes us from the beginning. Without it we would be inert, flaccid, flat. With it we have energy at our disposal; our motor is running. Though we have not yet fully engaged our gears, we are positioned to do so.

It is only with the passage of time that we will move toward fully moral action, haltingly at first, more concertedly as our powers mature. Parents, mothers especially, get early glimpses of these still undeveloped impulses, and can interpret them: he or she has a temper, is shy, is fearful, is venturesome, etc. Such is the God given equipment that will stay with us throughout our lives. However, these tendencies will develop by way of training, education, discipline, or lack thereof, and a youngster's proclivities will mature.

In their early stages, they remain orientations that lack full moral implications; their standing as good or evil is insignificant. A person at this level is not yet "up and running" enough to follow or disregard Christ; the young one is still at the (morally) crawling stage. None of these early manifestations of behavior is predictive of the moral status of a person, but only suggestive, and so there is a correlation with the early stages of viewpoint functioning in a corresponding way in such a young individual. To say of an infant that he or she has a temper is not a negative prediction, as if dooming a person to injurious outbursts, (since temper is neither good or evil), any more than good humor in a toddler is an undesirable indication that he or she will never develop a sense of determination and commitment. Rather, each is God bestowed equipment that will be activated when the time comes to begin the mature journey Godward.

These early signs of predispositions toward behavior often contain intimations of a vocation, understood as a calling from God. For vocation is not an alien element planted in the midst of one's life, proving ill at ease in a strange setting. Vocation indeed comes from elsewhere, but is designed to resemble a home-grown impulse or urge (just like inclination) often present in one from early on, and hidden amid tendencies in a person as if one of the native endowments; indeed, it has the potential to coordinate the other latent energies that are beginning to bubble forth. Nonetheless, almost native and innate as it appears to be (because so closely aligned with one's inclinations), vocation has an element of otherness about it, precisely because it is a call, coming from elsewhere, and from Someone else. It's like the call of a parent to a child playing in the yard of the house—a call that the child does not generate, but which he or she hears and integrates into his or her pattern of behavior quite naturally, as the child leaves the yard and enters the house. Or again, a parent may notice in the baby boy his penchant for building things with construction blocks or legos, or, in the baby girl, her fascination with constantly clothing and re-clothing her favorite doll. Are vocations latent in these examples, to carpentry or fashions?

Vocation easily mingles with inclinations to constitute a compound of energy that will supply a person ample initiatives for the remainder of his or her life. It is designed to endure to the very end when an accounting will be taken both of the talents one has received from God (Mt 25.14-30), and the call. For inclination/vocation, in combination, is a gift, complementing perspective, so that, together, they constitute the components that will fuel the moral agency of a person. There is more to consider regarding the development of a morally adept person, of course, but these are foundations without which the further components of morality will count for little in the final analysis.

A further role played by vocation in equipping the fully endowed moral agent is its personalization of the fundamental option. While all of us are given the same general opportunity of enhancing our inclinations through that special moment early on when God graces our existence by emerging at the edges of our lives (the fundamental option), each of us also receives a very special call (from God—the white pebble or amulet in Rev 2.17), not shared with anyone else, where this first instance of engaging God takes on the added feature of a personal invitation to each of us, adding a note of completion to the earlier encounter constituted by the fundamental option. While fundamental option, as a salient instant igniting a feature of our nature in one of its most significant experiences (the igniting of freedom), vocation enhances that basic tendency in much the same way that personhood enhances nature, by introducing a distinctive uniqueness separating one from the other. Vocation builds on fundamental option like grace builds on nature.

Given its importance, prospects of mistaking one's vocation, or deliberately following another one, are not to be disregarded. Just as abiding by a defective perspective possibly distorting the way one sees things can be deleterious, without necessarily being disastrous, so pursuing a vocation other than what one is called to do is an arduous undertaking, though not doomed to failure. Surely we have met someone whom we judged to be in a wrong vocation, such as a priest who should have been doing something else. Admittedly, such a turn of events presumes one is not following his or her strengths (inclinations). Nonetheless, there are multiple ways of moving ahead in life, just as there are various ways of transmitting blood to the failing heart. We recall the rich young man of the gospel, and wonder how he developed in later years, though there is no reason to think that his future was unhappy. (Mt 19.16-30)

The close approximation to vocation of inclination, as just mentioned, nonetheless acknowledges a difference between the two, to the extent that inclination is interiorly generated rather exteriorly produced, and inclination also occurs earlier in one's existence as an innate energy, while vocation usually occurs later on, personalizing one's endowments and gifts. But both are direction-oriented proclivities within oneself. It is in this setting that the fundamental option, also mentioned above, emerges, as a tendency percolating within a person, providing one an opportunity to make a foundational orientation of self to (or away from) God. This important moment is sometimes called the fundamental option. A later development among the tendencies underway within a person, it emerges in the same time-frame that the use of reason does in a young person. It is unique among our human orientations because it propels one beyond the fields of activity that earlier inclinations tend toward, and reaches out beyond to encompass one's entire expanse in this life, representing the very first thrust, generic though it be, of a young life toward or away from God as He first emerges into the field of one's awareness (or perspective). Fundamental option is the embryo of freedom, and freedom's first expression, coordinating with the incipient use of reason to bring God to bear upon one's whole life orientation. It is the first glimmer of freedom breaking through. At this juncture, the moral enterprise becomes full-blown and catapults one onto a new level of agency. The life of good or evil, the pathway to or from God, unrolls before one, somewhat similar to the

Cain and Abel event (Gn 4). It is an energizing event opening up vast new dimensions to the inner drives within oneself, like being on the edge of a large waterfall that will carry one into an entirely new adventure of motion and activity. It separates itself from the other inclinations of nature, functioning within the confines of nature, and reaches out beyond human nature toward or away from God.[2] Who knows whether this acme of human achievement is a product of God's grace?

The fundamental option is more than just inclination; it represents the advanced status of inclination as it morphs into freedom. And freedom is at the heart of the moral enterprise. Just as there is a gradation in the movement of one's mind toward that important moment of acquiring the use of reason, correspondingly there is a modulated trajectory in the development of inclination toward the mature status that is freedom. When reason and freedom come together, we are situated to begin the serious pursuit of moral agency under the aegis of God, and to struggle with the presence of moral good and evil before us. The basic option before God is initiated at this point, and can go either way. Generated from within, it differs from vocation, imparted from without. Corresponding to the growth in one's perspectival outlook on life, to the point where one can stand back and take notice of the viewpoints contending with each other as guides in seeing what lies before oneself, so a similar development occurs in one's tendencies, to the point where one can take ownership of those to be harnessed as an energy source for doing a task. At this juncture one breaks into an expression of freedom. It is a significant breakthrough, when one exerts control over these inclinations rather than submitting to the control they try to exert on one's behavior.

Once again, as with perspectives, so with these tendencies, there comes a point where one is able to master them on one's own behalf, rather than have them drive us on into behavior that will lack the potential for achieving much good or evil. It is at this juncture that we are on the verge of freedom. From then on, freedom is in position to assume a dominant place among the inclinations propelling us. The first significant manifestation of it in terms of the fundamental option can have its counterparts later in life. For there are likely to be several major turning points in one's life where one must come to terms with oneself in fun-

---

2   Sebastian MacDonald, *The Sacramental Roots of Human Freedom* (Lewiston NY: The Edwin Mellen Press, 2008), 36-45.

damental ways, especially if one leads a relatively long life. At these junctures, one must ascertain whether one is to be driven again by one's urges or to reenergize freedom by taking charge of them, making them serve his or her goals and purposes.

On these occasions something called conversion can occur. This is a major event, comparable to the fundamental option, a truly substantial transformation of the basic drive powering the way one's life was moving. Conversion is a premier instance of freedom at work. Given its cataclysmic impact on oneself, it is not likely to happen frequently. It is a rare occurrence. Moral theology is quite interested in the conversion process because of the promise it holds out for pursuing the good more vigorously, while correspondingly rejecting evil. It is mindful of the prominence it enjoyed in the preaching ministry of Christ, and of all the prophets before Him, concluding with John Baptist. Conversion is not easy. It is a fresh beginning, entailing a new moral evaluation of one's life, allowing one to correct what has become distorted or listless. While it may not be accurate to assert that one must be saintly in order to properly assess the course of action one must follow, it is certain that one must be alert to poor positioning due to perspectives and inclinations succumbing to bias and error. Conversion to the good is a way of reorienting ourselves after abuses of freedom (sin).

The scriptures are replete with examples of conversion, the most outstanding of which is that undergone by the apostle Paul on his way to Damascus as a fiery Jewish zealot seeking out followers of the new Christian religion (the Way, as in Acts 9.2, 19.23, 22.4) in order to capture and imprison them. Encountered in a remarkable fashion by the risen Lord (Acts 9.1-9, 22.4-16, 26.12-18), Saul became a changed man. His fundamental option toward God, obviously active in him throughout his life till then, was transformed into a vocation (or a different kind of vocation), effecting a conversion of life that made of him an equally fiery Christian protagonist.

In the last analysis, inclinations, like perspectives, are the raw material for mature moral activity, the first indications of which appear with the fundamental option. Vocation, as with the apostle Paul, can further enhance this development. Perspective and inclination are suggestive of the moral activity to follow, but not predictive or determinative. They are implied in an oracle of scripture: "Whether a tree falls to the south or to the north, wherever it falls, there it shall lie." (Eccl 11.3)

Chapter 3

Experience

Experience is the stuff which morality engages in guiding human agency toward goodness, amid threatening evils. Should there be a deficit of experience, there is inadequate material which moral evaluation can explore. That is why the use of reason is so important as the borderline because it is where/when morally significant experience accumulates—whether after the early stages of life, or before the later periods (when senility commences).

Experience is generated in large measure by perspectives and inclinations. But there are other elements, too, that enter into its generation, probably too numerous to enumerate accurately. This makes for some difficulty in gaining an adequate appreciation of experience. For, though we speak of it often, we do so with a certain lack of precision, so that each of us probably uses it slightly differently from how another employs it.

Those of us reaching the age of reason acquire a measure of experience, some more than others. Age accounts for part of the difference in this regard, with the presumption being that an older person has more experience than a younger one. But this is not necessarily true. For one reason, it represents a quantitative understanding of experience, overlooking a qualitative one, meaning that some kinds of experience (especially when morality is concerned) involve a value that is not commensurate with the time exposure that one has accumulated, for instance, in some specific area of human activity. E.g., a person's military experience may count for more, when it has involved actual combat, than another's, who has never seen combat, even though he or she has spent more years in the military.

There are other qualifications as well, bearing upon the pertinence of experience in morality, but there will be no attempt to itemize them all. For the purposes of this small book, it suffices to remember what has been said above about perspectives and inclinations (namely, they both have a premoral influence that is suggestive but not predictive of an agent's moral status; above, pp 12, 16) since they provide initial stages of gathering experience. But there is much more to experience than perspectives and inclinations provide. Nevertheless, their coordination and interplay (how we tend to frame things, and how we position ourselves toward them) certainly play a role in the accumulation of experience, which depends on their interaction.

There is a further characteristic of experience. Perspective and inclination, while significant components of experience, are both internal to the human person. Their functioning is foundational to experience only in view of their dependence on the context or situation surrounding a person. They suppose an element external to them. For perspective is a viewpoint on what lies beyond an individual, while inclination tends outward, leaning beyond the self. Experience is what results from the exchange occurring between a person and his or her surroundings. And there are other factors also which come into play, such as the bodily senses and their contact with the environs. These functions are central to experience as something interactional and relational.

Experience shares in the uniqueness contributed by perspective and inclination. That explains why no two persons experience a situation in exactly the same way. This is due, not to differences in the context enriching experience, but to a variance in the way someone frames the setting, and reacts to it. The cataclysm of 9-11 was the same external catastrophe for everyone present to it, but as an experience it was unique to each person there.

So with other human experiences: joy, sorrow, surprise, humor, anger, hunger, hurt, anxiety, fear, hope. None of these experiences occur identically in different individuals, even though the situations giving rise to them may be the same for each of them. As a result, the assessments of them, for instance, as morally good or evil, will vary. Similarly, even though the situation that one particular individual experiences remains unchanged, e.g., a childhood neighborhood, the experience of it, occurring when one returns there years later as an adult, will be different because of changes within us in multiple ways, including those of perspective and tendency. The frame of reference brought to bear on it after many years, in conjunction with corresponding tendencies in its regard, have, given the passage of time, been influenced by other situations over the course of time, such as other neighborhoods we have visited or inhabited, resulting in an enlarged collection of experiences that bear upon the way we reappraise what had been so familiar and well-known years ago. Thomas Wolfe noted this in his novel, *You Can't Go Home Again* (New York: Harper & Row, 1934).

Experience, in this fuller sense of the term, supplies what is lacking to one's merely internal perspectives or inclinations. Experience in this sense can improve our efforts, for example, at exploring a new environment, in which we find ourselves, so that it suitably meets our needs. In fact, through an extensive breadth of experience in examining other settings for ourselves, in ongoing efforts at bettering our situation, experience serves as a laboratory in which we can explore possibilities experimentally, on the basis of trial and error. Experiment often lies in the background of a rich experience, and frequently opens up new pathways for ourselves, especially when it becomes obvious that our native endowments, such as perspective and tendency, are not able to cope with a situation developing before us. Planning that relies only on native genius or personal endowments, but lacking adequate familiarity with the setting around oneself, is unlikely to succeed. But if it takes care to incorporate experience that is familiar with one's setting, planning is more likely to achieve its goal.

Experience accumulates what is becoming familiar and incorporates it into itself, so that it becomes the tried and true. It adds to our efforts an element of confidence and reliability based on "what works" in the circumstances in which we find ourselves. At times it is only experience with one's surroundings that provides the component needed to accomplish a task successfully. The internal constituents of a person, such as perspective and inclination, are needed components in any enterprise comparable to the moral task of doing the good, but if the linkage between a situation and the individual has not been adequately established, the likelihood of doing good and avoiding evil is notably diminished.

Experience is a time-honed asset. To one's native endowments it adds the element of efforts attempted many times over, to bring personal capacities into contact with one's surroundings, so as to effect their improvement, and our well-being. Educational institutions are sometimes willing to recognize the value of experience in a student applicant who may otherwise be lacking sufficient academic credentials to meet the requirements of a course, or a degree. Businesses often seek employees with experience as well as academic degrees. In these instances, the experience in question entails an added element (success/failure through trial and error) that can establish the qualification of a person to accomplish the task before him or herself.

That, of course, is at the heart of morality: to do something well (that is also good), as not only a faithful but also a successful follower of Christ. While the internal attributes of a person contribute to this task, exposure to the trial and error of dealing with one's surroundings adds a prized dimension that strengthens the likelihood of success in this effort. Experimenting with various ways and means can provide better ways of achieving one's goal, even a moral one, since accomplishment is not an incidental factor in revealing the true mettle of a moral agent. The scriptures provide us examples of how this component is esteemed. In the Book of Job (1.6-12) we note the agreement reached between God and Satan to test the latter's insistence that the status of Job as a truly virtuous man has not been adequately established, and so he should be tested by undergoing a series of trials and ordeals. Only this will establish his moral integrity as one seriously pursuing a pathway to God. It was only exposure to a challenging experiment that proved the moral worth of Job. Prior to this severe test, Job seemed to be a good man. After undergoing trial in the fire of temptation (a spiritual experiment), Job's moral integrity was established beyond a doubt by the reward received from God (42.10-17).

Jesus Himself submitted to testing in the desert at the commencement of His public ministry. He exposed Himself to hardship and temptation, in preparation for His great work of announcing the kingdom of God to be at hand. It was not enough for Him to be clearly incorporated into God's plan for Him until He had experienced the rigors of the desert as the crowning "proof" of having achieved His entry into the human condition. (Mt 4.1-11)

Experience, especially in the form of experimentation, in its trial and error phase, is comparable to temptation. It tests the inner worth of an individual by exposing him or her to outer circumstances that try one's genuineness and quality. It is a trial and error effort, where provision is made for error, only to expose and eradicate it, for otherwise it may have gone unnoticed as a possible future liability. But, once exposed, the opportunity presents itself for eliminating or at least reducing it.

God has utilized this process in our regard, from the very beginning. In the Garden of Eden we hear of the perfect man and woman in an ideal setting where there is strong likelihood that nothing but good will ensue from their sojourn there. But a trial and error element was built into this story, to test the quality of the undoubted rich inner endowments of the man and the woman. (Gn 2.15-17) And this test revealed something that was not otherwise evident in the early ideal conditions. Ever since this incident, temptation (a version of trial and error) has been part of the human enterprise, suggesting the value of experience in certifying the moral worth of each of us.

Experience, experiment, temptation, trial and error, can highlight the negative factors in human life. Theology has recently addressed the value of what it calls a negative experience, meaning an encounter with a situation that opposes what one values, and is trying to achieve. But this, and the other terms just cited, can stimulate something positive in our encounter with them. In the best scenario, they witness the contribution that setting and surrounding can play in helping us flourish, for they constitute a field of endeavor, where our true worth can be tried and proven. *Per aspera ad astra*. Achieving moral accomplishment without exposure to such challenges, on the basis of only our inner aspirations, is unlikely.

Another term, to be added to those already employed, is also useful in describing the venue where a fuller expression of experience becomes available to us: "the world". It is another way of referring to our surroundings. It is often an uncomplimentary term, especially within religious circles. We need little instruction alerting us to the world around us. It constantly engages our perspective and finalizes our inclinations. It is the place of encounter with others, who can challenge and call us out of ourselves, for weal or woe. But early on, "the world" had taken on a pejorative meaning for Christians, and for others as well, and in recent times this has taken on the hue and tint of further identification as the "secular". Contemporary church documentation has not looked kindly on the secular, tending to regard it as a value-free environment, at its best, and, at its worst, as a devious and distorting atmosphere, prone to lead a Christian astray. The practice of withdrawal from the world, and its secular influence, became an ascetical ideal in the ancient church, featuring anchorites, cenobites and desert fathers and mothers who left the cities of their time, where temptation lurked, and withdrew into the surrounding deserts. There safety was to be found, where one was not exposed to temptations, but was left alone, with his/her own resources, and a strong faith and trust in God. In such a setting these stalwarts proved their indomitable spirit, but they did so at the expense of impoverishing their experience through lack of interaction with the world around them.

This mindset inspired the origins of later developments called religious orders, congregations or communities, especially those monastic in composition, where a spirituality prevailed of caution regarding the dangers of the world and the secular. Given the remarks here about the role and value of experience in helping a person achieve a well-rounded moral capability to achieve the full dimensions of goodness (or evil) to which one is exposed, and the proposition that experience is incomplete if lacking exposure to the surrounding setting (usually characterized as the world, and the secular), there is need of testing the secular, for example, to evaluate both its danger for the moral enterprise, and also for its contribution to the effort at following the example of Christ.

The bible provides mixed messages on the secular, or, more precisely, on the world. There are certainly warnings about the dangers latent in the world (1 Jn 2.15-17, 3.19, 1 Cor 1.20, Gal 6.14) as well as fairly positive statements about the potential imbedded there (Gn 1.28-31, Jn 3.16-17, Acts 17.24). The first group of these references warns that the world, left to its own devices, is unadorned with the presence and action of God, and is a precarious place, so that the further we withdraw from any and all experience of it, the better off we are. On the other hand, recognition that the world has been touched by the hand of God helps us regard it as a fitting element in an experience that can help us make our way securely to God. The other set of biblical citations supports this appreciative assessment.

But it is especially the death of Christ on the cross, which we accept in faith as salvific and redemptive, that remakes and reconfigures the world, overcoming its sinfulness and waywardness, and freeing us up from undue worry and concern (such as we articulate in The Lord's Prayer). Experience of the world, for those enhanced by faith in Christ's death, becomes an advantage for us, should we call upon it. In fact, deprival of this kind of experience may well hamper us in pursuing goodness and godliness. Something similar can be said regarding the kindred word, secular. It is a derivative from the Latin word *saeculum*, which means "world". We show our esteem for it by concluding most of our official liturgical prayers with the formula: "...world without end. Amen". (*saecula saeculorum. Amen*). When extrapolated, however, from this context, and recontextualized into terms, such as secularism or secularization, secular becomes problematic. Recent church documentation has especially grown wary of "secularism", understanding it as a form of worldliness devoid of and inimical to the presence and action of God in the world. "Secularization", on the other hand, has come to be regarded more neutrally, as a descriptive term describing the world operating on its own terms and by means of its own devices and laws. It doesn't necessarily imply a repudiation of God's place in the world. It simply describes the course of worldly activity proceeding on its own terms. It arises out of the historical developments accompanying the history of the church, especially the reduction of the church's worldly power in the western world, thereby opening the door for secular forces to develop and assume responsibility for the temporal welfare of peoples. This is largely the case today, an era when secular states dominate the world scene, at least at the governmental and economic levels, while the Vatican has assumed the higher ground (evident in its interventions at the UN) as a legitimate and respected spokesperson for human, ethical and spiritual values and concerns.

This entire development coincides with the emergence of secularization. In the last analysis, we recognize the aptness of the observation of Terentius: "Nothing human is foreign to me" (*The Self-Tormentor*). This is a secular version of the sentiment ascribed to Jesus: "Sacrifice and offering you did not desire, but a body you prepared for me; holocausts and sin offerings you took no delight in. Then I said, 'As is written of me in the scroll, Behold, I come to do your will, O God.'" (Heb 10.5-7) In this digression on "the world" and associated phenomena, we continue to address experience, and its role in helping us become moral persons, by moving beyond our inner resources, such as perspective and inclination, to acknowledge the role that our surroundings and setting contribute to our moral capacity. Experience is often the "school of hard knocks", where our inner perceptions, ambitions and desires come into contact with surrounding circumstances, resulting in a honing and refinement of our moral sensitivity. Experience differentiates each of us one from another, both because we are differently gifted in our perspectives and inclinations, and also because we are variously positioned in our life circumstances. We cannot become fully moral persons, or completely prepared followers of Christ, if we lack experience. However, experience, as we will have occasion to remark in chapter five, offers no foolproof guarantee of achieving moral excellence. After all, there are bad experiences as well as good ones, just as there are distorted perspectives and misdirected inclinations.

Secular experience can be an important element in fortifying its value, even when there is question of religious/ethical concerns. The practice of slavery, for example, was countenanced by the church over a long period of time. The exposure of the church, through the breadth of its missionary experience, for example, to the evils of slavery was apparently insufficient to expose its problematic nature. Secular society, however, especially where democratic institutions prevailed, and freedom was esteemed as a fundamental value, saw more clearly and more quickly than the church, that the institution of slavery was an evil thing, and it took the lead in reducing and gradually eliminating it. The breadth of experience available to these secular sources contributed to a moral breakthrough in this matter. Broad experience such as this can be valuable in discerning the morality of situations.

It is a formidable task to face up to the challenges that experience presents us. But even negative experiences can have a silver lining around them. This has been brought home to us through Christ's death on the cross, a truly negative experience, if there ever was one. Nonetheless, the cross was the indispensable event positioning us to affirm the resurrection of the crucified Christ just three days after His horrible death. It is on the basis of this faith conviction of ours that we embrace the experiences before us, recognizing in them the potential to proceed *per aspera ad astra*.

Chapter 4

Experience as Personal

Experience adds a dimension to the richness of our moral aptitude that proves invaluable. We have considered it in terms of the expanded setting or context it provides, in addition to the performance of our perspectives and inclinations, especially in their early stages.

There are different kinds of experiences. Some are very extensive in their composition, covering long periods of time, or many different places. We usually have these in mind when we credit a person with having extensive experience. This suggests that he or she has lived many years and visited many venues.

On reflection, however, we see that this is a quantifiable appreciation of experience. As such, it is a legitimate and appropriate expression of experience. However, there is also a qualitative understanding of experience. At times, these two understandings of experience converge in the same person, making him or her a model of what an experienced person is like.

At other times, however, they don't coexist in the same person, but are found separately from one another. For example, one individual may be widely traveled while another may be much less so, having lived in or around his or her place of origin most of one's life. Nonetheless, such a person may manifest significant experience. The reason for this is likely that a qualitative kind of experience compensates for the lack of a quantitative type of experience. Such might be some very intense experiences one has encountered, close to home, which one has processed so that they have coordinated with that individual's viewpoints and tendencies, complementing their significance. This distinction in the kinds of experience that are of value is evident in terms of novelists, for example. One might compare an Ernest Hemingway, a world traveler whose overseas adventures provided him a rich source of experiences on which he drew in becoming a prize winning author, with the Bronte sisters, who stayed relatively close to home, but who found in their limited surroundings opportunities to explore deeply into the worlds of neighbors or acquaintances, with whom they associated, and who provided rich experiences which they could call upon in writing their novels. They too earned accolades for being superior writers.

The same holds true for everyone. We need experience upon which to draw, in order to excel, and this includes being a moral person. Experience entails contact with something in addition to acquaintance and interaction with the inner depths of our own lives. But that "something" doesn't have to be quantifiable. It can be qualitative. It is accessible in the books we read, in the talk shows to which we listen, in the films we watch, in the music we hear, in the art at which we gaze, in the conversations we join—all of which are qualitative episodes.

But of all the qualitatively promising experiences we have, few measure up to the potential inherent in the encounters and associations provided us by the persons in our lives (such as those who likely benefited the Bronte sisters). We recall the beautiful account in the Book of Genesis where a lonely Adam was portrayed, despite being placed in an idyllic setting, providing everything a man could want. God, perceiving that something was amiss in his life, paraded a variety of animals before him—quixotic creatures, each unique in its own way—but Adam, though undoubtedly finding them both entertaining and attractive, still felt something missing in his life, that would enable him to flourish. So God presented him a lovely creature like himself, the woman, and that happily satisfied Adam's quest for a fulfilling experience in the Garden of Eden. (Gn 2.18-25)

The introduction of Eve to Adam completed his experience, enabling him to engage not only something else beyond himself, but someone else. Among the various kinds of experience, the most significant is what another person provides. When person encounters person, its potential for intensity and richness is unsurpassed by any other experience, however attractive it may be.

We may hesitate, however, in agreeing to this, given some extraordinary situations that we have experienced, proving as valuable for us as any person in our life. For instance, we may have stood along the rim of the Grand Canyon, or gazed through the Hubble telescope at galaxies of distant stars, or admired Michelangelo's David or Moses, or thrilled at a Beethoven symphony.

This may possibly be true. But, for the most part, these are relatively rare experiences for many of us, whereas the experience of encountering another person is frequently available to us. It is important to have access to experiences that are meaningful precisely because of their potential to refine our moral sensitivity to a point where it provides us guidance along life's pathways.

For this reason it is helpful to review the role of the significant persons in our lives, whether family members, neighbors, fellow parishioners, fellow workers or schoolmates. They are the ones who most frequently provide us the experience that both supports and challenges us, testing the ethical metal of our lives. Life's challenges and opportunities, which contribute to our sense of morality, usually emerge in interpersonal experiences. This is true both for good and for evil.

In the last analysis, it would be difficult to recall any situation where a moral issue emerged in our life, disconnected from any person. This is true of the good experiences that we have undergone—the kind word, the thoughtful gesture, the helping hand, the generous gift, the word of advice, the loan of equipment or money, the loving care and regard—as well as the unfortunate and damaging experiences we have sustained—the lie spoken about us, the mean look, the deception against us, the personal injury sustained, the snub, the theft, the damage inflicted on our property, the contempt leveled at us. Persons are involved in all these experiences. If Adam would have lived without Eve, the quality of his experience would have been notably different.

Even the viewpoints and inclinations nestling within ourselves have a person-focus. But the present issue is experience and its significance for morality, because of its personal component. Experience of the impersonal is less frequently grist for its moral implications, especially in assessing the goodness or evil of our lives in terms spelled out by our relationship to God. This is because of the relational and interactive quality of experience, which is difficult to generate and sustain in terms of the impersonal, though examples just given above illustrate some exceptions to this, and especially the phenomenon of deep attachments to and affection for animals (pets).

Personal experience, however, is not all of a piece, as if one instance of it was as significant as another. Just as there are different kinds of experience, so there are distinctions in experiences that are personal. We don't consider the personal experiences with a salesperson, the postman, the boss or the teacher, in the same manner as we do a parent, a spouse, or a child. While there is a moral dimension to any experience we have of persons in our life, the more intense experiences occur in our interactions with the latter type of persons. The family is the hearth nurturing the most meaningful personal experiences, both for good, and for evil.

We will likely not experience elsewhere the sense of belonging, intimacy, oneness, community, and acceptance, that we do in the family setting, where the persons to whom we are closest generate an intensity of experiences not likely to be matched in other circumstances. This is an example of how a meaningful experience does not require numerous years lived or places visited, to contribute significantly to our sense of morality.

Family is the first and most important setting for notions of good and evil to spring up and grow. This does not depend on the intellectual or professional credentials of the family members, but on an entirely different set of familial experiences: the interactions and relationships that generate so much energetic and uninhibited impulsiveness.

Morality, of course, is as concerned about evil as well as goodness. In recognizing the potential for moral goodness within the experience of family life, we must also acknowledge a downside to such intimate bonding: nowhere else will we undergo the hurt, dismay, disappointment, anger, jealousy, perhaps even hatred, as occurs in the family. These are negative experiences that can undo and destroy us, but even at the nadir of this type of situation, a springboard effect can always leap into the breach, catapulting one upward out of the negative experience and back toward that earlier condition where a foundational kind of goodness prevails.

Among the positive familial experiences that foster a taste and relish for the morally good and beautiful is the married love between husband and wife. There is a depth, intimacy, exclusivity, fidelity and intensity to this particular experience unmatched in the world of personal relationships. The bible has utilized the meaningful expression that a man "knows his wife" in the marital embrace (a common translation of texts such as Gn 4.1, 19.8, Nm 31.17). This is a special kind of knowledge generated by sexual experience but enriched by a love, bonding and commitment not attainable anywhere else other than in the marriage bed. It is revelatory of the depths of a personal experience that is unmatched for its moral and ethical implications. For this reason, the bible, as just remarked, frequently refers to the marriage image in expressing God's love for us.

This kind of knowledge is an instance of another, related type, quite significant in its own way, though likely not of the intensity of the experience associated with marriage. This is referred to as connatural knowledge. It too is very experiential, with a notable interpersonal intimacy unique to it. Connatural knowledge is completely different from the knowledge we typically acquire in other familiar settings. It is not learned through purely mental processes, as happens in large part with the information acquired at school or in a book or imparted through a computer. It is less an enterprise of the brain and more one of the heart and other affective components of our activity. It is based on an affinity and attraction born of close association and involvement over a long period of time, to the point where one has acquired experience of a situation or a relationship (such as friendship) that instills knowledge of the inner working of another person, or of a process (such as farming or raising livestock), or of an exercise or routine like dancing or athletics to the point that it has embedded itself into one's sensitivity in such a way that one "knows" instantaneously, without reflection or deliberation, that something is developing well or poorly, or someone is happy or disturbed, or some action or omission is good or evil.

Experience is the essential ingredient for connatural knowledge, especially personal experience, such as a doctor's awareness of a patient's condition. We call it connatural because it is less an acquisition from outside and more an interior growth. It can't be forgotten. It is very much like conscience. It is difficult to disregard, and it generates response mechanisms in one possessing it, which reverberate throughout our system. It becomes a way of life, such as a mother's relationship with her infant.

The emphasis given here to personal experience, as over against other kinds of experiences (which have their own value too) cannot fail to draw attention to one Person in particular, the experience of Whom surpasses that of all other persons. That is God. God is a Person. In fact, in our Christian tradition, we acknowledge that there are three Persons in God.

So we extol the superiority of the divinely personal in the experience that is intimately bound up with moral issues of goodness and evil, thereby recognizing that there is a hierarchy within the range of persons who feature in our experience, and that this bears significantly upon our moral sensitivity.

Earlier, we noted the special features of the experience associated with the persons comprising the families that nurtured and formed us, and rightly so. But above and beyond them, there is God, Whose pervasive influence in our lives affects everything else. Paul Tillich had spoken of God as the ground of our being.[3] This is a profound insight, but it has an impersonal ring about it. We need the added dimension to our experience of God recognizing "In Him we live and move and have our being". (Acts 17.28)

God is well positioned to be part of our personal experience, given the intensely personal expression God enjoys as three persons, Each of Whom shares fully in Divinity, but Each in His own way. When we speak of personal experience as superior to other types, we can do no better than to recognize the uniquely interpersonal experience within the Godhead: Father, Son and Holy Spirit. Each of them is God precisely through inter-relating with One Another, not as if there were three gods, but as one God, and therein lies the Mystery.

The opportunity available to us to experience this richness of personhood within God provides a heightened and intensified instance unrivalled in other personal experiences. It exposes us to dimensions of goodness which we have not encountered before. Whatever we have already experienced, in terms of love, harmony, acceptance, forgiveness,

---

[3] *Theology of Culture* (Oxford U. Press, 1964), 127-132.

is magnified by interacting with God. By reading the Bible as the Word of God, we come to appreciate how He has entered deeply into human experience across the ages, in the manner of a Friend, the epitome of all personal relationships.

He has awaited our fundamental option for Himself, and has issued a call/vocation to us, seeking to engage our experience for the remainder of our lives, into eternity. He has gifted us with faith, a kind of connatural knowledge, enlightening us about Himself. We fall short in our appreciation of the part personal experience plays in morality if we fail to take account of God's role in it. Without this experience, the human person merely stands at the threshold of what experience can be, especially in its dimensions of moral goodness and evil.

Chapter 5

The Church

For all the prominence that God enjoys in our lives, it still remains that He is far above and beyond us. To speak of our experience of God may unduly diminish its meaning, in view of our acknowledgment that His mode of operation in and around us far surpasses our human modes of interaction. But, fortunately, we have faith to facilitate our experience of Him.

And faith enlightens us about another medium enabling our relationship to God. This has assumed an institutionalized form that is at hand to facilitate our experience of God. This is the church. The church is an instance of faith mediating God and ourselves. From our vantage point, it is both God's representative, mediator and spokesperson in our life, and also our advocate and helper before Him. Some of us have relatively easy and quick access to the church, and have experienced its role on our behalf, over many years.

The church is close to God's heart. While a human phenomenon that is not in any way divine, it has an extraordinary capacity for bringing God into our lives. Its presence to us extends over key moments of our existence, and will remain so to the end of our days on this earth. The church is ever present to us.

Some among us have a love-hate relationship with the church. We treasure her constant reminder of God's loving care for us, and of the ways in which He shows His concern for us. Her sacraments, her devotional practices, her presentation of the word of God in homilies, instructions and other media are cherished by us. She teaches us how to talk with God in prayer.

But we very much dislike her "haggling" with us, as she keeps after us for our faults and failures. She disturbs our conscience, reminding us of what we would rather forget. She asks for our money, and we sometimes feel we don't get a satisfactory return on our contributions to her. She formulates almost impossible ideals at which we are to aim, making us feel totally inadequate. All of this we dislike.

Admittedly, she is present to us, especially by her sacraments, at all the key moments of our lives: our birth, our reaching young adulthood, our need of spiritual nourishment, our search for forgiveness, our marriage, our periods of sickness, our search for inspiration through her ministers who mediate our worship of God. It is usually her priests who represent her at these key times in our lives. Troubled as these men can occasionally be, they are indispensable.

Many of us take the church for granted, as we do with so many things in life that are near and dear to us. Since she can't force herself into our lives against our will, we can afford to shuck her off with relative impunity. Her clergy don't constitute a police force who can enforce her programs on us. So the church exerts a mixed influence reflecting both a human and a divine dimension. At times we respond too casually to her in view of her human side, reducing her to just another institution that we can call upon at times of need, but disregard at our convenience. On the other hand, there are those special moments when we stand in deep need of her ministry in our life, holding out spiritual support that we truly value. This combination of her institutional/spiritual composition befuddles us, especially in these recent times of scandal, complicating our experience of her as something human, yet exuding the divine.

It is worth exploring how each of us personally experiences the church in our life. Are we too deferential, idealizing her as if she could do no wrong, so that, when she does, we either try to deny it, or excuse her? Or are we too critical, forever looking for occasion to fault her, diminishing or even dismissing her role in our lives, whether it be her teaching or her ministrations? One helpful criterion in assessing our experience of her is in her capacity as "mother church", for this urges us to employ the same criterion in evaluating her that we employ in assessing our own mothers. We know that our birth mothers are not perfect. We're aware of their faults. But this recognition is couched in something more pervasive and deeper than any faultfinding which may flit across our mind: our love for her. If we love the church as our mother, it may well happen that critical judgments about her dart into our thoughts about her, while such criticism leaves our affection for and loyalty to her intact. She still maintains her influence on our experience of God, others and even ourselves, and she continues to earn our respect. It is a sign of a truly mature relationship to the church when our devotion and commitment to her remain, even amid the disagreements we may have with some of her teachings and positions. The inability to adopt this posture should be a cause of concern for us.

For the church to maintain significant influence on our moral agency, as believers in God and followers of Christ, however, we do need at least occasional interaction with her. Is not relationship at the heart of experience? If our relationship with the church is sporadic, or diminishing, our experience of her as a significant influence will gradually subside. This same distancing can occur even with our birth mothers. Should force of circumstances remove us at some distance from them, over a long period of time, chances are that a diminished interaction with them will dilute the maternal influence over us.

The phrase "mother church" goes a long way toward suggesting how to de-institutionalize the church, to the point where we can personalize her. This humanizes our experience of the church. Otherwise, the more we identify the church as just another agency, of which too many already complicate our lives, the more we regard her as an alienating factor for us. Pope Benedict XVI speaks movingly of this in his first encyclical, *Deus caritas est* (nn 30a, 31a), where he distinguishes social services conducted by the church on behalf of the needy with those performed under the jurisdiction of state government. He suggests that there is more of the human touch in the first than in the second. This points to the need of a human face on any helping institution, especially if it purports to resemble the human face of God, as Jesus so well provided at a time when some were visualizing God in an overpowering fashion.

The genius of one of her key roles in our life is that of sacramental administration, because it interrelates with key experiences of our lives.

Especially the sacrament of the eucharist, coupled with the church precept about Sunday mass attendance, combines to insert us on a regular basis into the rhythm of a spiritually nutritious encounter with God, and this is bound to become a foundational experience for us, in conjunction with the corresponding injunction about repenting any serious sin impeding our worthy reception of the eucharist. This, in turn, leads us to consider another of the church's sacraments, that of reconciliation/confession. The sacramental combination of eucharist and reconciliation constitutes an experience leading to an enrichment of personal morality, by confronting any significant moral evil that will offset the moral goodness at which we are to aim.

Apart from these sacramental moments, another major moral experience available from the church is her teaching ministry. The weekly homily at Sunday eucharist is a primary way available to the church for refining our moral sensitivity. Unfortunately, the experience of the Sunday homily by people in the pews continues to lag behind its potential for providing an excellent experience of the church as teacher, despite a new style of preaching encouraged since Vatican II, with its emphasis on the power of the biblical Word of God. Serious efforts must continue to make preaching a truly nurturing source of moral sensitivity.

However, the heavily scriptural orientation now encouraged in homiletic preaching does fail to communicate an adequate moral message to the faithful, providing an experience that is more generic and exhortatory than practical and instructional. Despite this problem, the church ceaselessly reminds people about the Decalogue, the beatitudes, and the law of love and forgiveness, most of which seems to be readily accepted. But when it comes to her social teaching, where moral experience does rise to the fore, a contentious reception frequently emerges from this endeavor.

This is not so much the case when it comes to addressing what are called socially conservative issues in American society (abortion, homosexuality, contraception, cohabitation, embryonic stem cell research, physician assisted suicide). People are responsive to the church's competence and experience in these areas. But when dimensions of social morality are proposed that reflect a standard liberal or progressive set of issues (the death penalty, warfare [especially nuclear combat], excesses of capitalism, defense of labor unions, a living wage, universal health care coverage, immigration, and government-sponsored programs on behalf of the poor), then even usually loyal Catholics frequently balk at this teaching. One of the few social issues of this type, gaining increased attention from the church, and attracting support across the spectrum of her membership, is care and concern for the environment. The disparity in responsiveness to these particular types of socially ethical concerns seems traceable to the longstanding experience of regarding some of these issues as legitimate church concerns, whereas others of them are experienced as secular affairs falling outside her moral competence. This generates a frequently heard complaint that the church should stay out of politics. As a result, whereas some readily accept church admonitions on matters of sexual morality, for example, they balk at its pleading for a more humane public policy on immigration.

Consequently, the experience of church teaching is a mixed accomplishment. To resort to the "mother church" image again, with an experiential reference to our birth mothers, it is similar to our acceptance of advice from our natural mothers about best practices in the kitchen, while dismissing their competence on machinery in the garage.

Another area where the church significantly enters our life experience as a mother is in her teaching us how to pray. Prayer is talk with and to God. It is as indispensable for us as any conversation is. We know from experience what a major event it is in the life of a baby to formulate its babble into a word, and eventually into a series of words. The ability of the baby to correctly name people and things is a triumph. This integrates the child more snugly into the heart of the family, establishing the first indication that he or she can entertain exchanges and relationships with the people who really count. Much the same is true with mother church. She socializes us to experience companionship with some very important persons, beginning with God. On occasions of attending church, whether for sacramental worship, or devotional practices, an enriching moment is realized when we address God Himself, without more ado. It would be more than an anomaly that the current total absorption with the convenient experience of cell phone conversation would relegate conversation with God to an insignificant experience.

We can gain an enriching appreciation of the dimensions of the experience associated with the church through her history, beginning with St. Paul and his vigorous preaching ministry. The phenomenon of conversion, mentioned earlier when considered as an instance of inclination (pp 16, ff), early on became a common experience in the lives of many people, thanks to the efforts of Paul. The missionary thrust of the church provided a significantly new kind of experience for many peoples, at both the individual and the national levels. It resulted in the significant growth of church influence, and a corresponding problem for the powers that be, which viewed it as a threat. Jesus' preaching about the coming of the kingdom gave off troubling signals to leaders of nations, as did His message that the law, while still to be revered, no longer proved adequate to the full dimensions of the kingdom that He proposed.(Lk 16.16) Shortly after His death, the experience of a church expanding into the Gentile world caused significant concern to the Jewish members of the early church.(Acts 15) And, as the church developed geographically, its cultural influence grew apace, as it acquired hegemony in the Roman and Byzantine empires, leading people to experience her as dominant in practically every dimension of life, at least in the western world. No experience in life, private or social, escaped the influence of the church.

Unfortunately, this did not necessarily bode well for the church or its members. Acquaintance with church history alerts us to the many moral (social) evils existing at the very time the church exerted its greatest influence in peoples' lives. This brought about the gradual demise of esteem for the church, and eventually the Protestant Reformation. The fallout resulted in the diminishment of church influence in the world, and likely the current mindset among many that the church is better advised not to overstep her boundaries. Unfortunate experience had a role in this development.

Acquaintance with church history and the experience it involved apprises us how the church was wrong in her reaction to practices such as slavery, torture (the Inquisition), and science (the confrontation with Galileo), yet this sorry saga has proven to be a surprising factor leading to, among other things, the growing practice of making up one's own mind about moral issues, that is, following one's own conscience.[4] And, contrary to expectations, the church has regained moral preeminence in the contemporary world, so that even those professing no loyalty to her whatsoever, look to her guidance on moral issues, recognizing the rich wisdom embedded in it. As remarked earlier, it is one thing to dis-

---

[4]   In his novel, *Souls and Bodies* (New York: Penguin Books, 1990), 118, David Lodge suggests that the many dissidents, among the laity, from the encyclical of Pope Paul VI, *Humanae Vitae*, led many of them into the practice of forming their own conscience in matters of morality.

agree with mother church; but it is another thing to loosen our attachment to her to the point of disrespecting her. When Pope John XXIII published his encyclical letter, *Mater et Magistra* (1961), some tried to divide their response to it in terms of *Mater*, si, *Magistra*, no. This was an unfortunate example of accepting the church as mother, but not as teacher, and represents a bifurcated experience of the church in one's life.

But even in instances where disagreement with church positions occurs in certain areas of social morality, this is more desirable than situations where the experience of the church as a guide in the public spheres of life is dismissed as valueless. For, the citation from Terentius applies to the church: "Nothing human is foreign to me." (pg 23) It remains that the church is the face of God in the contemporary world, and reflects His all-encompassing concern about human affairs, so that everything human counts for something in her sight. To experience church in this way provides a heady appreciation of what the church is all about.

In recent times we have struggled with the question: can one experience salvation, without the church? We have come to recognize that, in some form or fashion, she will indeed play a part in securing everyone's standing before God. The explicit recognition of (or experience of) her by each and every person is not the central issue, but rather the influence she exerts, one way or another, in working to accommodate everyone's spiritual and moral standing before God. This is why Pope Benedict XVI has often expressed concern about the demise of Christian influence in Europe. He realizes that there still remains a lingering presence, a residue, of church-inspired values permeating the continent after two millennia of her influence there, and that this constitutes an experience that has permeated the psyche and outlook of those living there, regardless of whether they are Catholics or Christian. This spiritual tonality will disappear from the continent, should the experience of church subside. For, while God has outfitted everyone to come to terms with basic moral values, (Rom 2.12-16) the inroads of original sin, in its various guises, necessitates the influence of the church to clarify what otherwise remains a nebulous and unclear experience of the moral code, at least partially, whereby to guide our lives. In this sense, we need the experience of church for access to the moral values that lead to our flourishing in this life, and, to the extent that salvation is embodied in this finely honed experience of culture, civilization and progress, the church is needed for salvation.

We might well ask ourselves how the church's presence and role in the lives of family, friends, acquaintances, government, business, education, health care, poverty reduction, racial relations, peace and justice, and environmental concerns makes a difference?

In the last analysis, we best calculate our assessment of church experience in terms of giving and forgiving. The church is a giving assembly of people. We may lose sight of this, amid the many pulpit announcements about special collections on behalf of the church. When all is said and done, we are engaged in giving, not only through the taxes we pay, but also by the intervention of the church on these occasions—and usually for worthy causes. But even more than this, we primarily experience the church as giver by her role in transmitting God's blessings on our lives. These endow us mainly through her sacraments, practices and instructions. Nor should we forget the tangible benefits that have accrued to us in her ministries of education, health care, and social services. So, both spiritually and institutionally, she benefits us by her gifts. Our awareness of this provides us ample reason for gratitude, as a prominent part of our experience of church. We epitomize this response of ours in the eucharist, whose very meaning expresses gratitude to God for gifts received.

By way of extending the word "giving", we can illustrate another experience of church, in terms of her "forGIVING" role in our regard. To the extent we are aware of the impact that sin has had on us, we quickly come to appreciate forgiveness as a premier gift. The dimming of ideals, with the passage of time, the lessening of enthusiasm, the growth of selfishness as we focus on our own dreams and ambitions, the reluctance at giving and helping, the growing suspicion of others, the overlooking of gratitude, the increase in self-centered concerns, our lashing out at those we perceive as threatening our security, our growing imperviousness to injuries caused by our omissions and oversights—all these accumulate into a heavy burden upon us. Sinfulness becomes an all too familiar experience of our lives. The comfort that we take in knowing that "everyone is doing it" gives way before the church's reminder that forgiveness and reconciliation are available. This prods us to review our behavior and conduct, so as to experience the church as a gathering of forgiven people, an Easter assembly keenly appreciative of the gift bestowed by the newly risen Christ on Easter Sunday evening: the power to forgive. (Jn 20.19-23) Of all the gifts the risen Christ might have bestowed on that memorable night, He chose His favorite: that of experiencing forgiveness. Among our many experiences of church, this lies at its center.

For all these reasons, when we experience the church, we experience the face of God. She stands in for Christ, continuing the ministry He began among us. This is why we acknowledge her as the body of Christ, and see ourselves as members of that body. This is mystery, eluding our understanding, but not our experience. We accept it in faith, recognizing further that, if we are truly Christ's body, then Mary too assumes a special relationship to us. For she gave birth to His body. She has thereby given birth to the church, becoming Mother of the church. This extends the use of the term "mother" to both Mary and the church: Mother Mary, and mother church. Both Mary and the church are holy, yet both are mothers of sinful members, namely, ourselves. But we are in good hands with mothers such as these. Thanks to them, we have access to a rich experience redolent of moral goodness, and forgiveness for our failures.

Chapter 6

Culture

Another major area of experience, constituting an influential set of surroundings with which we interact by way of our inner perspectives and inclinations, and develop our sense of the morally (in)appropriate, is culture.

It is plausible to think that culture is even more pervasive in and formative of our experience than the church. For not everyone is a member of the church, at least in an actively aware manner, while everyone is a participant in culture, in some conscious form or fashion, though, admittedly, not the same culture. For there is a variety of cultures, though today, due to globalization, a convergence among them seems underway.

But, regardless of the traits of any specific culture, each culture provides the ingredients for an experience, constituting a venue with which to interact and dialogue, in ways to be described in what follows. We gather an impression of what culture is by reflecting on its meaning in specific fields such as biology, or medicine, whose practitioners develop what they call "cultures", consisting of various life forms, that grow and mature in a nurturing milieu, usually within laboratories. Such a scientific culture is a milieu where minute elements interact, germinate and generate. A scientific culture is an intricate system nourishing life forms.

Not dissimilarly, culture, as proposed here, is also understood as a fertile context in which other kinds of life forms generate and develop. These are often of an artistic, academic or technical kind, that provide the setting in which other remarkable achievements are brought about. An early historical form of this is religious culture, whose practices of cult or worship provide the very word that gives birth to the term "culture". Cult is a mode of venerating some higher being or god. Cult is an act of obeisance to such a god, whereby the worshipper abases him or herself before a superior being. Cult is at the center of a religious setting, where God is offered worship and adoration by the human being.

The setting for this is usually a special place, variously called church, temple, mosque, etc., and specific rituals on how to act and what to do are followed. Usually a leader, such as a priest or minister, rabbi or imam, officiates at a cultic procedure. Engaging in cult at a worship service is considered both inspirational and beneficial for the practitioners.

This kind of activity has continued down the ages, at times featuring examples of cultic actions that are indisputably disturbing, and even immoral, such as the biblical references to temple prostitutes (1 Kgs 14.24, 2 Kgs 23.7, Hos 4.14) indicate.

We sometimes rank the quality of life in an ancient civilization by the culture that characterized it. We regard as great cultures those that enriched its participants with a sense of appreciation for the finer things of life, such as generating traits like generosity, kindness, humaneness, compassion, care and concern, all of which make for better human persons, enjoying sustainable living conditions. Such achievements register the moral dimensions of a culture.

We refer to Greek and Roman civilization as examples of superior types of culture, given the recognition they afforded values such as truth, goodness, and beauty. These cultures produced monuments that have perdured until our own time, as architectural masterpieces with statuary of high quality. At the same time, we are astounded at evidence of savage cruelty among them.

There are equally impressive signs of high culture found in Egypt, Turkey, Syria, Israel, Jordan, China, India, etc., and, within our own hemisphere, such as Mexico, Central America (the Mayan and Aztec achievements), Peru. All of these witness to the soaring heights that the human spirit can reach, given the proper environment to support these expressions of native genius, especially from the ruling elite.

In general, people of such advanced cultures give indications of comparable codes of moral conduct. This doesn't imply that virtue prevailed and vice was eliminated. But it does show the human capacity for lofty ideals and aspirations, even if they were inconsistent in conforming their behavior to such expressions. And it explains why culture has come to be valued by religious and moral leaders in society, who regard it as an important ingredient in preserving society and the body politic.

Moral theology, too, does well to heed the culture of its surroundings, and to take the measure of its merits and failures. For there is much good to be discovered there, that can prove helpful in supporting its advocacy of what is morally good, despite elements of moral evil that are also in evidence. Moral theology needs all the help it can muster in providing guidance on the path to a good life—and onwards to God.

At its best, culture represents a blend of experiences contributing to the improvement of the human person. In addition to the art and architecture just mentioned, it includes various kinds of writings (plays, poetry, history, philosophy, science, religious texts, commercial documents, legal treaties and covenants, recipes, health manuals), music, crafts, pottery and cooking utensils, coinage, jewelry, tools, weaponry, carvings, etc. In short, anything contributing to the comfort and overall well-being of the members of society is a mark of culture, and this includes the customs, practices and laws whereby people structure and organize their lives, so that they proceed in an orderly fashion.

One element more or less common to any review of cultural artifacts is beauty. Beauty is often an overlooked factor among the things that contribute to human well-being and flourishing, despite the fact that it has always been closely linked to the true and the good, the perennial staples of humanness. For beauty has a harmonious influence on human society, soothing and calming it. It has an inner power to placate imbalances, disorientations, shapelessness, inappropriateness—in brief, the ugly. Hatred, hostility, and violence are among the "hard" human reactions that are often expressed in an explosive manner, the epitome of ugliness. Beauty consists of balance and proportion, and tends to realign and rectify whatever gets out of line. That is why the bible calls upon beauty to express its understanding of God. (Ps 50.2, Wis13.3, Sir 42.23)

Especially in the Christian tradition of both east and west, there has been a reliance on beautiful artifacts, such as music, images and statuary, to express our worship of God. However, this has also been a bone of contention at different periods of history, such as the condemnation of Iconoclasm heresies in earlier centuries, and the Reformation position in the sixteenth century, make clear, when certain Christian groups thought it highly irreverent and irregular to attempt depicting holy things in human ways, no matter how artistic. Another instance of this is found in Jewish synagogues and Moslem mosques, which, while often outstanding architectural achievements, carefully avoid any depiction that might be considered an attempt at representing the divine. Rather, both groups prefer to use symbolic and geometric forms to express their religious aspirations regarding the divine.

Religion and its accouterments have always been regarded as a prize jewel, among cultural achievements. There are indications of ancient religious practices excavated from archeological digs, which expose much about the cultures of which they were a part, often in a very formative way. If culture is a web of meaning around which peoples' lives have centered, it is especially the religious features of that meaning which have contributed a significantly humanizing quality evident among them. Some of the most beautiful artifacts discovered amid the ruins of these cultures are religious in nature. There is a symmetry between the beautiful and the truth in these cultures, helping us learn about what peoples of long ago knew and believed, in the way that they worshipped. Exposure to, interaction with, and experience of these facets of culture have shaped and formed civilizations.

The Vatican has maintained a treasure house of artistic treasures from cultures of long ago. This has been a source of scandal to some who think that the vast wealth embodied in these collections could and should be channeled into more productive and helpful uses than museums. Yet these museums and libraries are a witness to the capacity of the human spirit to reach levels of excellence that some are too eager to deny. These older cultures have had their finer moments. Just as the church has always maintained there is a natural law available to the human person as a guide for discovering moral truth and goodness, and touts the brilliance of some of the ancients for expositions on this law, so she has also shown her admiration of other cultural achievements of long ago, as a further witness to the powers of the human spirit to grapple with the beautiful, and thereby with God, its author. She values these examples of human experience. What an impoverishment it would be for the human spirit to be deprived of the Vatican-preserved masterpieces of Michelangelo, Raphael, Da Vinci, Fra Angelico, Giotto, etc., nearly all of whose art was religious in nature. The Sistine chapel lifts not only the eyes, but also the mind and heart to God, by way of the beautiful.

It was this same mindset that inspired the burgeoning European monasticism of the dark ages, to establish libraries and scriptoriums to house, protect and meticulously reproduce ancient manuscripts that served to bridge the ages. Some monks developed masterful artistic skills of iconography in transcribing these parchments, beautifully illustrating them.

It is especially in her own liturgy that the church has combined decorum of movement and music, fostering a variety of cultic rites and ceremonies embodying her sacramental activities. In general, these fall into separately divisible branches of the church: the one being Roman or western, the other Byzantine or eastern. But, within each of these two major categories is a variety of more specific liturgical forms. Within the familiar Roman rite, there are the Ambrosian and certain religious order variations, while, among the eastern rites, we find the Alexandrian or Coptic, Syrian, Armenian, Maronite and Chaldean forms—all exquisitely choreographed forms of worship. The religious sensibility of many cultures lay behind these multiple rituals, and all illustrate the meaning of the dictum: *lex orandi, lex credendi* (The rule of prayer is the rule of faith-life).

The church's liturgical experience is a notable instance of the connection between religious action/rites and codes of behavior and morality. This is seen in the orderliness so prominent in these worship services and the harmonious collaboration of different liturgical agents in effecting proper behavior and conduct. The convergence of beauty and goodness is more apparent here than in most other spheres of cultural experience.

Several years ago, Samuel P. Huntington wrote *The Clash of Civilizations and the Remaking of World Order* (New York: Simon and Schuster,

1998). He might well have said "the clash of cultures". He had in mind, of course, the current setting where Islam and the west are engaged in a spirited attempt to influence the direction of world events. Each represents a venerable culture (that of the east, and that of the west), boasting a proud record of achievements. It remains to be seen whether the clash he describes is an accurate portrayal of their relationship, or whether it is a transitory and perhaps ultimately mistaken interpretation of an actual convergence that is underway, in broken continuity with the earlier exchange between Islamic and Christian cultures prevailing in the 11th (Avicenna) and12th (Averroes) centuries, when they both shared, and profited by, the wisdom of an older Greek culture, discovered in the ancient manuscripts that these Islamic scholars also made available for western thinkers, such as Thomas Aquinas, and which were cherished for so much that was found there of profound truth, goodness and beauty. It was an instance of transcultural experience.

Later, in the 16th century, Mateo Ricci, SJ, became involved in another cultural convergence developed under his missionary tutelage, as he sought to integrate Chinese religious practices into Catholic ritual. He had come to experience and appreciate the beauty in Chinese culture, such as its burial rituals, whose compatibility with Catholic worship services he tried to establish. Ricci regarded these unfamiliar modes of cult as deeply expressive of the universal meaning of death, always a wrenching experience. Unfortunately, the "Chinese rites controversy" resulted in the snuffing out of this promising missionary attempt, and delayed an appreciation of how new cultural experiences can lead to an expanded appreciation of beauty and goodness.

Prior to Ricci, of course, was his great missionary predecessor, Paul the Apostle, who showed himself a master of two cultures (Jewish and Roman/Hellenistic), and who displayed no hesitancy in utilizing them in the exercise of his missionary ministry, as when he adroitly appealed to his Roman citizenship so as to gain transfer of his pending court trial to Rome, thereby avoiding a possibly biased Jewish trial (Acts 25.10-12). Paul obviously appreciated and valued the fairness of the justice system prevailing in the Roman culture.

The topic of "culture" has grown within Catholicism in recent years. Vatican II's Pastoral Constitution, *The Church in the Modern World* (1965), devoted considerable attention to culture in Chapter II: "Proper Development of Culture". Pope John Paul II instituted the

Pontifical Council of Culture, in 1982. He realized the impact and import of culture, from his Polish interfacing with Communism, to convey meaning and value in a much more impressive way than school education alone could do. Responsive to culture's powerful impact on contemporary sensibilities, he coined the phrase, "the culture of death", (*Evangelium Vitae*, 1995) to articulate his concern about the inroads of death-dealing procedures becoming ever more readily acceptable in contemporary societies, with abortion leading the way. In recent years the term "culture" has been attached to many phenomena, both negative, such as the drug culture or the culture of greed, and positive, such as a youth culture, a vocation culture (mentioned frequently at the Montreal International Vocation Conference in 2002), a media culture, etc. Culture is the breeding ground of experience where moral (dis)values are generated.

It is likely that people mostly derive their sense of what is morally good and evil, acceptable or unacceptable, largely from the culture surrounding them. At the present time there are so many ways in which the surrounding culture impinges on the inner sanctum of our perspectives and inclinations. Most of these influences are electronically powered, and it is difficult to identify them, since new ones appear on the scene with such rapidity. Western culture especially is saturated with influences that heighten one's awareness both positively (by pointing out the evils of sexism, racism, war and violence, environmental pollution, militarism) and negatively (by depicting the vaunted advantages of sexual freedom, homosexuality, stem cell research and abortion, pornography). It looms as a moral challenge to ground one's moral experience in largely church-acculturated teaching, education and family training, when, for so many others, this is likely not often the case.

However, we need not passively succumb to the negative features of the surrounding culture. Like Mateo Ricci, we can take an aggressive, missionary-like stance toward it. This will certainly lead us to address and assess the influence of the secular on our experience. While we cannot distance ourselves completely from it—nor should we even want to do so—we can critically engage it. A missionary mindset will lead us to recall Thomas Aquinas' dictum that grace builds on nature. (*Summa Theologiae* I, 2, ad 1) An appreciation of nature is a step in the direction of understanding the secular, often by way of the potential within culture. God's grace does not aim at dominating nature, but at improving and transforming it. Time spent on trying to neutralize nature, or the secular, is poorly spent. We do better to adopt a missionary attitude toward our surroundings, cultivating their positive potential, as the church, for the most part, has done with culture over the ages. In doing so, there is promise of enhancing the moral tone of us all. Briefly, it's a matter of experiencing culture, interacting with and relating to it.

While some of us may look back at the '60s, especially in this country, and judge this decade to have been the worst of times, riddled with libertinism, riots, the Roe vs. Wade Supreme Court decision, assassinations of prominent persons, and its disoriented flower children, we should not be so traumatized by the admittedly moral deviations that were so obvious, as to overlook and forget a Pope John XXIII, the Second Vatican Council, the election of the first Catholic president, the growth of the Civil Rights movement, the energizing music of the Beatles, Peter, Paul and Mary, the antiwar movement, Rachel Carlson, and so many other developments and persons that the culture of that era generated and fostered, which helped to make this period the best of times. There were instances of the good and beautiful in the culture of the '60s serving as the yeast in the dough or the mustard seed in the ground, that nurture us today. That raucous experience involved the birth of a culture so latent with potential that it influences our life today.

Chapter 7

Conscience

Influenced as we are by vital and impelling forces, such as the church and culture, and significant persons (God especially), while immersed in multiple other experiences as we wend our way through life, it is heartening to realize that we are not mere directionless corks at the mercy of these various experiences, but that we can and do have resources of our own regarding the conduct of our lives, in addition to the perspective through which we look out about us, and the drive of our inclinations toward what we see around us, as described in the first two chapters.

For while it is true that we come to learn much about good and evil around us from our rich experiences of people we encounter (God especially), of church, and of culture, we have within us a weighty anchor to stabilize us amid the vortex of all these experiences to which we're exposed: conscience, which is capable of holding its own amid these influences. Conscience joins perspective and inclination as an inner resource that addresses these other factors, reacting to them, and imparting a highly personal stamp on the moral stance that we eventually adopt.

Conscience is as unique to us as are perspective or inclination. It is likely that no two consciences function in the same manner. For conscience is a judgment we make, whether prior to an action, or subsequent to it, either sanctioning what is happening or has happened, or repudiating either instance, and it does this in conjunction with our personal inclinations and frames of reference.

It's important to note that it is a judgment. Unlike perspective, which is a viewpoint, or inclination, which is a tendency, conscience is a judgment that either clearly supports a course of action, or warns against it. Conscience tends to be more concise and focused than either perspective or inclination. Though there are times when it can be fuzzy and even confused about a course of action facing us, it normally tends to proceed with firmness and precision. It is uncomfortable dealing with situations impairing its judgment regarding what to do or not do. In its trajectory underway within us toward doing or omitting something, conscience comes at the end of a series of interior operations and procedures, aided by one's perspective on something and a corresponding inclination in its regard, and influenced by other experiences as described above. It is one of the last steps we take before doing or omitting a deed.

Because it comes toward the end of a process, tentativeness and doubt are less probable, since it is likely they would have been dealt with earlier on, enabling conscience to be decisive and clear. But this is not a certainty. There are, frequently enough, cases of a doubtful or hesitant conscience, as to how to finalize the question as to "what to do". These are the cases in which conscience benefits by an abundance of experience, beyond our own limited outlook on things, and basic proclivities. When, in this scenario, a person is on the verge of reaching a judgment about a mode of behavior, such a one will be helped by past experience with a similar situation, when we made a conscience judgment which seems to have been a correct one.

As a judgment, conscience is a product of the cognitive part of our internal operations, rather than of the volitional phase. But it serves as a bridge between them, because it is a cognitive or mental procedure that is in service of an action. However, conscience is not a thinking process engaged in reflection, but rather comes at the end of a series of other procedures intent on thinking through the steps leading up to an imminent action. It assumes a position that is on the verge of action. So, while undoubtedly sharing a mental orientation reflective of one's perspective, and likely influenced by the basic inclination operative within a person, it works further down the line toward the actual doing or omitting something. Whereas perspective is more unfocused, and tendency is not yet operational, conscience judgment is like a laser beam shining straight at the launch position for full-blown agency.

Conscience, then, is not designed to think through problems, or to speculate, or to weigh the pros and cons of a situation. That process has already taken place. It is proximate to action, but not the actual deed doer. That belongs to another part of our moral activity, in which inclination becomes operative: the performance part of behavior. Conscience confines itself to making a judgment to do this or avoid that, or, if it's operating in hindsight, to judge that we should not have done that, or should have done this. But, as indicated above, conscience isn't always successful at being so clear: at times it's caught in a genuine ambiguity, and doesn't know how to come down with a judgment about a situation. In that case, one can't act in good conscience, since one might be making a wrong judgment, that will then engender a wrong action. For one to go ahead and act in such uncertainty signals that he or she doesn't care about the possible evil in question. This already sullies the situation. Hence the dictum: never act with a doubtful conscience.

So it is obvious that conscience operates in a very confined area; its field of performance is narrow, in comparison to the freer play that perspective or inclination enjoy. Conscience judgment is a step beyond the process of comparing possibilities, and is in the countdown stage of launching an action. It operates past the earlier phase of scouring the field of possibilities; it locks in on one precise thing to do or avoid, the immediate step giving the command: do it/don't do it. So while conscience is enriched by all the preliminary steps taken, right up to its very doorstep, it moves beyond these into its own territory.

But, despite all the preceding help it has received, conscience can still be wrong. However, it never produces its judgment about doing or avoiding something, under the guise of wrongness; that is, it doesn't judge: do this because it's wrong, or skip this since it is evil to do so. No, it always operates under the guise of correctness: do this because it's the good thing to do, or skip it because it's proper to omit it. Acknowledging this, though, doesn't nullify the wrongness of the judgment, and all of the wrong background information leading up to it. A man's wife may be dying of a painful ailment, and his conscience judges that the good and proper thing to do is to alleviate her suffering by administering a lethal dose of medicine. That is an erroneous conscience call that may be dependent on some background information to that effect, but which is also erroneous.

However, one must always follow one's conscience judgment, so in this instance the husband incurs no sin in the sight of God (though he may be subject to a different judgment in the court of law). We must always follow conscience, even an erroneous one, noting however, that, while a certain conscience always proceeds under the supposition that it is right (while, as a matter of fact it may be wrong) a wrongness can still be involved if this conscience judgment was instigated by a person's past blameworthy mode of behavior, such as insufficiently consulting about the matter, or deliberately seeking advice from less than reputable sources.

The upshot of this mandate to always follow one's conscience, right or wrong, doesn't necessarily imply a psychological problem is involved here. In fact, freedom is always presupposed as an accompaniment of acting in accord with conscience. When that is not the case, then there may be a kind of determinism forcing a conscience judgment on oneself, resisting any attempt to instruct it otherwise (as some kinds of scruples exemplify). This could be a pathology needing attention.

Given this kind of predicament, we have to be concerned about our conscience; we shouldn't take it for granted, as if it were an automatic response in need of no help. It can veer off and go the wrong way, leading us toward evil under the guise of good. Conscience is designed to guide us toward doing the objectively good thing. But we're not helpless before our conscience, as if it ruled the roost. True enough, like perspective and inclination, we're born with it; it's a given that becomes operative as we mature. We don't gain it by reading a book or graduating from school or observing how others act.

Nonetheless, even though we don't generate it within ourselves, we can certainly influence and change it, as we can our perspective and/or inclination. Reading a book, listening to a lecture, observing how others behave—all of these, while not instilling a conscience within us, can instruct, or misshape, our conscience. So, in view of the possibility of its making wrong judgments, it is in our best interests to educate it.

Experience that has been acquired in appropriate settings can endow conscience with a number of scenarios that prove instructive and constructive, though experience, too, can be malformed and so be an unwholesome influence on conscience. The task at hand is to glean experience from interaction with morally commendable and upright people or situations so that conscience can be well shaped. Experience is the best of teachers.

Such experience encompasses culture, church, and persons (especially God). It is exposure to these which contributes to the formation of judgments about what is morally good, or evil. However, we have the striking case of Franz Jagerstatter during the Second World War, a married man with a family, an Austrian living under the Nazi regime, who could not conscientiously collaborate in any way with the Nazis, and who was willing to take the consequences of his position, which entailed the loss of his life. In his case, his experience of the surrounding culture, local parish church, family, friends, etc., was not supportive of his conscience judgment that the Nazi regime was immoral, and that he could in no way collaborate with it. As a result, he suffered arrest, imprisonment and ultimately execution, as a result of following his conscience.

A different outcome of the impact of experience on the formation of conscience is described in the Japanese novel *Silence* (London: Peter Owen Publisher, 2007) It concerned Jesuit missionaries in Japan during the 17th century, whose activity caught the attention of Japanese authorities. The ruling class disapproved of them, and began a persecution, both of the missionaries and the faithful who had become Catholic, many of whom underwent a cruel martyrdom for following their conscience, enduring great sacrifice for the sake of the faith. One of the missionaries, however, began to wrestle with his conscience, as it underwent the experience of subtle reeducation, eventually reaching the conviction that he could in good conscience agree to the stipulations of the authorities, and he apostatized from the faith. This saved him from a martyr's death, and established him as a collaborator esteemed by the government. This story depicts an experience that wrongly influenced conscience, to the point where the missionary gradually came to judge apostasy as an acceptable and correct course of action—a possibility that was repugnant to him early on, but that, with the passage of time and the influences brought to bear on him, apparently morphed into a the right judgment for him to make. Who is to know his standing before God?.

Both of these cases illustrate the uniqueness of conscience. We had already noted the highly personal nature of perspective and inclination, both of which also exhibit this quality, as when several of us, viewing the same thing, nonetheless see it differently, or incline toward or away from it, each in his or her own way. A similar response typifies conscience, when morally upright persons (family and friends) can judge the selfsame action differently, as in the case of Franz Jaegerstatter, and in that of the Japanese missionaries, the integrity of whose conscience judgments led them down different paths in dealing with their profession of faith before persecution. This uniqueness of conscience judgment, evident in differences about the same issue, has come to the fore in recent U.S. presidential and congressional elections, when some candidates, even Catholics, have adopted pro-choice positions, while the others have not. Similarly, American Catholic voters have split in their support of these candidates. Short of accusing those voting for a pro-choice candidate of violating their conscience, or possibly acting out of ignorance (whether culpable or not), we recognize in this example well intentioned and presumably informed persons reaching different conscience judgments about the very same thing.

Another well-known historical instance of a conscience judgment taken in almost solo fashion, and certainly against the tide of public opinion, such as it existed in those days, was the "Here I Stand" manifesto issued, April 18, 1521, by Martin Luther as he presented his case—and his conscience judgment—before the authorities of the Catholic Church in the 16th century., at the Diet of Worms. It was likely a lonely stand. Luther was conscientiously convinced of his moral uprightness; many others were not. But, with the passage of time, as we look back, we appreciate the problems Luther saw in the church of the time, that issued forth in the resolute judgment of his conscience, challenging the powers of the day.

Conscience is primed to judge action or omission, whether it reaches this judgment accurately informed or not. It is relentless, following its course of action whether we want it to do so or not. It's an automatic response, so to speak. We prize conscience as one of God's gifts to us, as we make our way through the maze of moral issues confronting us on a daily basis. It represents a bastion of internal strength amid confusing and contentious times. Though usually resolute and decisive, it is malleable, as already indicated. We can influence the way we want it to go, for good or for evil, though this is a process that takes time.

There are helps beyond ourselves that can bear on it, and steer it toward the morally good, some of which proceed from the hand of God, especially God the Holy Spirit. But there are also helps, that is, influences, veering us toward the morally evil. We benefit by the gifts of the Holy Spirit, especially that of counsel, which endows us with the facility of discerning the right judgment to make amid perplexing situations. In addition, there is the virtue of prudence, designed to bridge the gap between perspective and inclination, that is, between how we see things, and how we are inclined to conduct ourselves. Prudence bears upon action as intently as conscience does, but with the added advantage of being more than just judgment. Prudence also weighs issues, compares them, and enriches one's move toward action with reasons justifying the move. Prudence is more flexible and more ample than conscience, and acts the part of its tutor.

Conscience is a precious commodity to treasure. We must indeed follow it, but must try to form it in the best way possible. The older Catholic practice of a frequent, if not a daily, examination of conscience, witnesses to the esteem in which it was held. A similar examination is called for in approaching the sacrament of reconciliation. Unfortunately, the diminished practice of this sacrament has reduced the importance of conscience in pursuing goodness and Christ-likeness. The neglect of conscience is a liability for us. For the variety of moral experiences arising out of contemporary culture exerts a potent influence on moral standards about goodness and evil, before which only an alert conscience can survive as a beacon of light, ready to interact with our surroundings as a helpful experience responsive to the Catholic moral code. While, in times past, there may have been excessive attention given to examining conscience, the current murky milieu calls for a strong beam illuminating the path before us. Care is needed to maintain conscience in prime condition.

5

Chapter 8
Negative Experiences

Experience broadens our acquaintance with good and evil, for weal or woe. Without experience, we would be babes in the woods, when it comes to coping adequately with the goods and evils that inevitably confront us. In other words, without experience we could be hampered in being good Christians, Catholics, and promising followers of Jesus Christ.

We have explored various aspects of experience in the preceding chapters. Nearly all of this treatment has assessed experience as a positive process in helping us appreciate the kind of influences to which we are exposed in pursuing our lives.

But a more complete picture of experience must also note its liability, in addition to its advantages. It can be as deleterious as it can be supportive. Instead of presenting itself as a positive element in our moral/Christian journey, experience can be a negative one.[6] There is such a thing as a negative experience, and interaction with it can be as much a challenge as a help. The question arises whether even this kind of experience can contribute to our flourishing and growth.

When experience is positive, it is not difficult to see in it an opportunity. The possibility for self-improvement is present. Up till now, in this

---

[6]   Edward Schillebeeckx, *God the Future of Man* (New York, Sheed & Ward, 1968), 155-6.

handbook, we have regarded experience as an asset in achieving moral adeptness. Aware that in recent times the term appreciative inquiry has come to the fore, we may have in it another way for regarding experiences as stepping stones toward moral improvement and flourishing. It fortifies our effort not to disregard or take for granted experiences of every type, by highlighting the advantage(s) they offer us. This approach offers an alternative to what has been the more common way to improve our lives, that of concentrating on the problems facing us, so as to find a way to solve them. For a long period of time, Americans especially have prided themselves on their problem-solving ability, in the effort at gradually improving their lives by discovering, and then correcting, problems, one at a time. This appeals especially to scientifically and technically minded persons, whose acquaintance with and access to available ways and means of proceeding has provided them advantages, and often success, in this effort.

In large part, a negative experience usually means a problem, of one kind or another. The preceding chapters have not focused on these, but rather have taken the approach of appreciative inquiry to various kinds of experience, noting the opportunities they afford us for becoming morally good persons, whether they emerge in the context of culture, of church, of conscience or of other persons, especially God.

But we know that life experience is multidimensional, with as many downs as ups. So it is to our advantage to acknowledge the undesirable features of experience, recognizing their negative quality. In doing so, we are not rejecting them as opportunities to improve our lives. In fact, we have just admitted that they have instigated at least some of us to adopt the active stance toward them of problem solving. Many of us rightfully pride ourselves on the skill of doing so. There is an optimism at work here: every problem solved improves our chance for a better life.

We can profitably address two particular problems that come to mind: sin and suffering/death. Though distinct from each other, they are closely related, especially within the Christian tradition. They constitute major problems which have never been satisfactorily solved in this life. Nonetheless, Christians believe that there is at hand, in their tradition, pathways towards solutions (so to speak), that make of these negative experiences something promising for us. That is to say, we can salvage or redeem these setbacks to see them as stepping-stones along the way of moral development.

In the first place, faith instructs us that neither sin or suffering/death is endemic to the human situation. That is to say, neither of them is necessarily linked to what it means to be human. God did not intend these negative experiences to be an inevitable part of human life. The opening chapters of the Book of Genesis instruct us otherwise in this regard. (Gn 3.17-19)

However, they made an early entrance into the human condition, and so seem to be part of our human fabric. The bible, in detailing this, suggests a certain priority in their relationship: sin came first, followed by suffering and death. (Rom 7.9-11, 13) This is a religious interpretation of the sequencing at work here. Cultural anthropologists may have another explanation of this situation, based on their observations of the life/death process underway in all forms of existence. But Christians believe that God made us for happiness, and, despite our early waywardness, which seemed a major problem in God's program for us, God found ways and means of adjusting the situation, so that happiness still remains a viable goal and destiny. This is a new scenario, in which the sin experience, coupled with suffering/death, plays an important part.

There has been a realignment of possibilities for us, whereby a positive experience (an opportunity) presents itself to us amid the very negative experience (a significant problem) of sin and suffering/death. As a result, moral goodness/happiness is still within our reach, but by way of the problems brought on us by sin. These entail suffering/death now becoming part of everyone's experience.

This includes even Jesus and Mary, despite the fact that neither of them ever sinned personally. Yet their humanness associated them with sin, as we have come to know in the person of Jesus Christ, Who underwent His Passion and death by reason of our sin, not His (Rom 5.8-11). Likewise, His mother, of whom Christians profess her sinlessness, underwent suffering, especially during the traumatic ordeal of the crucifixion, whose linkage to sin (not hers, but ours) entered into her experience. So they both underwent the sin experience vicariously, in the suffering and death that was their lot too.

Thanks to the Passion, the problem of sin has been addressed for those gifted with faith in its saving power. But its linkage to suffering and death remains as a vestigial and very negative experience, and so a malingering problem for all of us. So, while problem solving is in evidence here, it is more positively assessed as appreciative inquiry exposing opportunity describing human and Christian life. While sin and death still face us, now, thanks to faith, we understand them as stepping stones toward moral goodness.

However, while the sufferings and death of Christ on the Cross help us to interpret the true dimensions of moral evil/sin, we continue to regard both sin and suffering as almost inexplicable (Rom 7.13-25). But thanks to faith, we catch glimmers of both the problems and the solutions before us.

This scenario explains why, in addition to Christ and His mother, others, even the best, among us suffer. We learn of the inner turmoil of a Mother Teresa of Calcutta, and wonder at a woman of her sterling character and utter dedication to the destitute undergoing such an experience. Or, in trying to comprehend the shoah endured by over six million Jews, we ask how this could be. And as we deplore the ravages and abuse young children sustain from so many sources, we struggle at what these innocents face. But these play out against the background of the Man on the Cross. We have come to appreciate that the intensity of these sufferings in no way indicates sin or evil on their part. At the same time, none of this suggests that the silver lining around life's dark clouds makes the darkness any more acceptable.

There is no reasonably satisfactory way of working ourselves through these conundrums. We must fall back on faith to alleviate otherwise unintelligible misfortunes. Such are negative experiences, in the full sense of the term. They are problems of the greatest magnitude, which have plagued human history from nearly the beginning. But, in a strange, inexplicable way, these problems can germinate their own solution. Encountering moral evil can be the genesis of moral goodness, though this will certainly not always be the case.

To illustrate this, we observe a corresponding phenomenon, but on a vastly different level, about an encounter with one type of suffering called pain, that is to say, physical pain, such as a burn suffered while cooking at the stove. Our instant reaction to this very negative experience/problem is immediate: we reach for relief (that is, salvation, or remedy). This occurs by a victim withdrawing his/her hand from the hot stove. This is a rather primitive example of the principle of reaction against a very negative experience. One instantly engages the situation, and at almost the same time seeks relief from this painful (and so, evil) experience. How good a soothing salve feels. This process, operative at one level of our existence, is transferable to another level of our experience, as when someone, enveloped in the suffocating suffering of loneliness, reacts by seeking relief in new relationships; again, a move initiated at the prompting of an evil situation, but leading to its opposite, the goodness to be found in companionship. And similar dynamics occur at other levels of the human enterprise, as when *The Fortune 500* magazine, in its April, 2009 issue (vol 165, no 5), reported on new enterprises gotten underway by people refusing to become discouraged when the economic downturn was severe, by proving creative at this time: another example of a problematic experience for many people giving rise to new opportunities that were quite positive.

The spiritual sphere of our lives reflects this scenario, in the process of conversion, earlier referenced in chapter two on inclinations. Conversion usually involves a similar turnabout, sometimes from a dissolute, miserable life, replete with suffering, to a vigorous reaction in another direction, as a person changes the direction of his/her life by moving emphatically toward the good. A problem-plagued existence can generate its own solution. These examples of negative experiences morphing into positive ones, which the conversion process especially illustrates, indicate the potential in negative experiences to develop into positive opportunities.

In the case of conversion, however, breaking the stranglehold of sin on our lives is no guarantee that suffering will diminish. If that were the case, our confessionals and many helping professions would be frequented by those seeking relief. Similarly, any revival of prayer in a person's life, following upon conversion from a very unhappy life, is no guarantee that a reduction of suffering will follow in short order. God has His own ways of addressing our problems, and the diminishment of distress is not always His primary concern.

In fact, often there is a dawning awareness that suffering, despite its status as something evil, nonetheless plays a part in God's plan for us. We can hardly avoid coming to this conclusion as we revert to the memory of Christ's suffering on the cross. The combination of His innocence and the intensity of what He underwent is a vivid reminder that suffering, which, endured with love, enabled Him to bring untold blessings upon the world, proves to be a gift in disguise for us all. It suggests that a positive experience can result from a negative one, convincing us that problems can generate their own solutions.

This had been abundantly evident in Jesus' life, during which He devoted so much of His attention to the sufferings of those He met along His way. His miraculous healings of the disabled and the disturbed won Him fame and following among the people. (Lk 9.11) Many of His miracles had to do, not with physical liabilities, but spiritual ones, especially evident in the exorcisms of the demons that had taken over the lives of so many. (Mk 1.34) His life and ministry became blessing and gift fashioned out of the maladies afflicting those around Him. By often linking His healing of physical suffering to an exhortation to avoid the spiritual suffering of sin in the future (Mk 2.5-12), He manifested His awareness of the sin-suffering connection and their mutual interaction: the genesis of one was the inception of the other, and attending to one effected a response to the other.

Suffering works a major benefit in our lives when it leads to a confrontation with whatever fault, failure or sin may have brought it about. But whatever sin may lie at the root of one's suffering is not always a personal sin of the one suffering. The suffering of Jesus on the cross, and that of Mary at the foot of the cross, witness to this. Furthermore, there is often another kind of sin behind the suffering afflicting us. It might be described as social sin. It represents distorted structural or institutional frameworks, resulting from the misshaped mindsets of those in power, which work havoc on the lives of the innocent. We think of social settings such as the mass starvations of people across the world, their bondage to inhuman working conditions, their succumbing to pandemic diseases like AIDS, their victimization in war zones, their struggle to migrate to more humane living situations.

These are negative experiences familiar to us all. While a sin component, often of a social or corporate nature, may be linked to some of them, we recognize other factors accounting for them. But nothing prevents us from viewing them all as problems, and, in doing so, to see in them the makings of a solution. Thanks to expertise developed in handling problems, we have a relatively good track record in addressing them. It is not helpful to overlook the import of seeing these as negative experiences, since it may expedite the prospect of viewing them in the light of appreciative inquiry, and so see them as opportunities from which good can be drawn. We know that suffering will always be with us, but we also need a conviction that human ingenuity has achieved significant success in its reduction. The secular world, for all its own moral blemishes, has many triumphs in its repertoire, and we should acknowledge this, and take advantage of the opportunity to address the sufferings Mt 25.31-46 describes, lest we be guilty of the serious fault of omission that was so roundly condemned in that parable by the king, before whom we all are to take our last stand. On that occasion the sin-suffering connection will be called to our attention, as well as the opportunities life provided us to be of help to those in need.

The church also aligns herself with the effort at addressing the sin-suffering linkage. While we ordinarily don't describe her efforts in this regard as problem-solving, as we do with secular institutions, we recognize the impressive manner in which she has carried on the ministry of Jesus on behalf of the disadvantaged and the suffering. The sin-suffering linkage among these people has not deterred her social ministry. Her sacramental system does devote itself to the inroads of sin in human existence. Several of her seven sacraments spell themselves out in sin-related terms: baptism washes us of the original sin so as to incorporate persons into her membership; reconciliation heals subsequent personal violations of our covenant with God; the sacrament of the sick clearly suggests the linkage between illness and sin; the eucharist is a sacrificial offering to God atoning for sin. Indeed, were it not for the very negative experience of sin, we should be deprived of the wonderful opportunity to savor the goodness of these sacraments.

It is likely for this reason that the church is much less prone to articulate her ministry among us in "problem" terms, than to think of it as "opportunity" to continue in this day and age the ministry of Jesus. The church is keenly aware of the sin-suffering linkage as a fundamental experience among her membership. They are both negative experiences that she doesn't run away from, since her entire membership, to some degree at least, is marked by these major problems. She is actually constituted to deal with this anomaly of leading back to the straight and narrow those of us who constantly wander off course.

Chapter 9

Compassion

The linkage of suffering to sin, as treated in the previous chapter, strikes a chord in the mind and heart of believers. There is ample reason to fear suffering, despite its capacity, especially under conditions that faith provides, for engendering unexpected goodness in life, as was also suggested in the last chapter, and as will be further explored, from another angle, in this chapter.

It is a safe conjecture that no one likes or relishes suffering. We would worry about anyone who did. However, we see the rationale of those who bring suffering on themselves, not for its own sake, but as a byproduct of something else that is worth doing. An obese person will submit him or herself to a rigorous diet in the effort to shed some pounds—and this involves a measure of suffering, or at least hardship. Would-be athletes undergo demanding physical routines to get in shape for some contest, as they submit to a training program that involves its share of discomfort.

So some measure of good can be associated with suffering. This becomes more evident if we shift attention from the physical aspects of suffering, and look at another dimension: the spiritual. There are instances of people willing to entertain suffering in their lives, not as a byproduct of something else they are trying to achieve, but as something good in itself. Such is the case when one experiences compassion.

Compassion is highly experiential because it is thoroughly relational. We can't exercise compassion in solitary fashion. I can't be compassionate with myself. Compassion is always outward reaching, to another who is suffering, and is usually interpersonal, that is, between two individuals, though a communal experience of compassion, on the part of several persons addressing the same suffering situation, is not to be ruled out. Its association with evil, (that of suffering) can be readily comprehensible to several, the moral goodness of whose reactions to it stand in stark contrast with it.

Compassion is numbered among the virtues that we revere and extol in our Christian tradition, though one need not be Christian to admire its expression. Indeed, not only is it a virtue, but, as will be proposed here, it is the primary virtue in the Christian repertoire of virtues. Under its influence, suffering undergoes a metamorphosis as a positive experience, diminishing its status as a negative experience and problem, while attracting attention for its potential to elicit an appreciative inquiry into it as an opportunity for pursuing goodness.

As just suggested, compassion is notably relational. It unites two persons in the experience of suffering. At times, an expanded understanding of compassion is operative when used to include other life forms, especially animal, such as an injured dog, rabbit or bird, the sight of which engenders a surge of responsiveness to it. Certainly, this is both genuine and good, and not to be belittled. Nonetheless, given the absence of a human component in these instances of suffering, the potential for the full experience of compassion is diminished in these instances.

In recent congressional hearings on the suitability of Judge Sonia Sotomayor to be a judge on the U.S. Supreme Court, several of the senators were, because of her background, quite concerned that empathy would play an excessive role in her rulings from the bench, since it was construed as an emotional orientation that would taint the strict legal interpretation of the law, advantaging one party, to the detriment of the other. Possibly so, but, then, empathy and compassion are different.

For compassion, unlike empathy (or sympathy), requires that the experience of suffering be shared by both parties, not just one. This is what is unique about compassion, that it is based on a shared experience. This doesn't mean that the sharing has to be of the identically same suffering in a given instance. But it does require that there be an experience common to both parties of sufficient quality to cement the kind of bonding that identifies compassion. If the suffering undergone by one of the persons is minor while that of the other is serious, sharing the full experience of compassion is less likely to occur. An exception to this, however, is the compassion of a mother for her child. That frequently does involve, objectively speaking, a minor impairment on the part of the child, but this doesn't prevent the mother from manifesting a full-hearted compassionate response to the young one, who easily senses it. A powerful biblical example of the mother-child bond in suffering is found among the exploits of the wise Solomon, who was approached by two women disputing over which of them is the true mother of a baby that they bring to his attention. When his efforts at settling their dispute are not succeeding, Solomon asks that a sword be brought to him. He then proposes to cut the baby in half, giving each woman a portion of the body. When one woman exclaims "no", give the child whole and intact to the other, Solomon realizes that she was the true mother, for the obvious compassion she displayed for the infant. In his wisdom he recognized the evidence of compassion as a reliable sign of motherhood (I Kgs 3.16-27).

The suffering involved in compassion can be any one of several kinds: physical, mental, emotional, spiritual. It can derive from different sources: interpersonal relationships, familial surroundings, a health condition, economic loss, impairment of reputation, a significant failure, a bitter disappointment, etc. It is pointless to assess suffering on a scale in an effort to judge its significance. Each of us reacts differently to suffering, so that one of us may respond strongly to this kind of suffering, while another vigorously reacts to another kind. Indeed, at times it is difficult to ascertain the presence of suffering, so deeply embedded has it become in a person. Suffering is unique to each, and can be extremely personal.

But, precision in judging the nature and gravity of suffering is not a prerequisite for compassion's presence. However, it is true that the focus of compassion is to be found less in the one receiving it, and more in the one extending it. But there is no need for the latter to engage in an analysis of the situation before extending a compassionate outreach.

Compassion is a form of love for another. It is an expression of comfort, support and consolation to one who is suffering. It is triggered by suffering, without calculating the worthiness of the sufferer, or the nature of the relationship between the persons, or even the degree of grief, in appreciating what constitutes compassion. Rather, the significant factor in the formation of compassion is that both persons must share in the experience of suffering. It is similar to lighting fire from fire rather than a matter of spontaneous combustion in a solitary manner, where the pain of fire, for instance, would be accounted for only in terms of one person. Rather, an exchange takes place between two persons, with suffering shared by both.

This is important for understanding as an experience: it must be mutual, relational. There are facsimiles of compassion, such as empathy and sympathy, which are certainly commendable because they too respond to a suffering person. But they are one-way extensions of help, proceeding from one person to another. But compassion is a two-way exchange, not in the sense that each person mutually extends a helping gesture to the other, but in the sense that a bonding occurs between two persons in a suffering each has experienced. A sympathetic person, for instance, can be quite helpful and supportive to a sufferer, but his or her outreach is not fueled by personal suffering, but is generated by some other factor, such as the feeling of concern at the sight of another who is suffering. This is obviously a very good thing to do, and needs nothing else to constitute its goodness. But it is not compassion.

In certain helping professions, personnel are warned, in fact, not to get involved in the suffering of those they are trying to help, because the experience of being drawn into the anguish of another to the point of identifying with it can unduly influence the kind of objective analysis and problem solving that someone in these professions needs, in order to accomplish his or her tasks well.

The special component of compassion consists in its equally requiring an experience of suffering on the part of each person. That is its typical characteristic. It is this particular kind of bonding that distinguishes it from that between one needing care and another bestowing it, which, as just indicated, best functions apart from such sharing. It is this kind of similarity in suffering between the compassionate person and the sufferer that accounts for its identity. Only this gives a ring of authenticity to the remark by one to the other: "I know what you are suffering." This comment is resented by the suffering person, who is led to respond: "No, you don't", unless it is a case of compassion, when a connatural awareness prevails on the part of both giving legitimacy to the response: "Yes, you do".

Compassion, then, is an expression of love. Of course, such can also be true of empathy and sympathy. But, given that there are degrees of love, with the higher form of love being mutual, bestowed by each on the other, then, empathy or sympathy are not an instance of that kind of love. While each of these can be a genuine expression of love, it is one-way love, from provider to receiver, with the two parties occupying different positions in the relationship of bestowing care and concern. There is also a love of gratitude, where the energy goes the other way, from receiver to provider, consisting of a genuine and profound welling up of thanksgiving in the sufferer for help bestowed, for example, by a professional person, such as a nurse, or a fireman risking his/her life to aid a fire victim. But the kind of love, comprising a shared experience of suffering, is unique to compassion, making it different from other types of love, even superior to love of enemy (Lk 6.27-36), since this latter love need not involve mutuality. Love of an enemy is obviously a magnificent manifestation of love, highly praised by the Lord (6.35), but it may not generate a corresponding love in return. That is, it may fail to become unitive and binding, and can even result in rejection. An enemy who is loved can prove spiteful and contrary, by way of response. Not so with compassionate love, which is unitive to the point where almost one person, one "I", results from the bonding that ensues. The compassionate person enters so deeply into another's suffering that it makes the verbal articulation of feelings unnecessary. A kind of connaturality becomes operative here, that is, a kind of knowledge born of experience where insight and appreciation is generated in such a way that it can be said that the compassionate person knows by way of inclination toward the sufferer, resulting in a kind of union, and the other person realizes that.[7]

An interesting feature of the kind of love expressed in compassion is that it is an abiding capacity; it is always available to one who has suffered, not only for this particular fellow-sufferer, but for any suffering person. That is why it is a virtue, and not a passing fancy. It is a per-

---

[7]   Thomas Aquinas speaks of this kind of tendency in the *Summa Theologiae*, II-II, 2, and the phrase *pondus amoris* ("the weight of love") was used to describe this experience familiar to those in love.

manent endowment and perfection of a person. A compassionate person is, as it were, ready and willing on a 24/7 basis for a mutual exchange with any suffering person, in such a way that it generates a loving response in return. This trait of compassion is not necessarily true of even the mother-suffering child relationship, to the extent that her response is based, not only on the suffering of the young one, but also on the fact that it is her child that is suffering. It is quite possible that, before an instance of someone else suffering, she may not experience the mutuality of compassion, in a manner sufficient to involve her with that stranger, with the same kind of intensity as with her own child.

Compassion is a significant achievement on the part of a person, not precisely because it indicates that one has undergone suffering him or herself, but rather that this experience has humanized an individual with a sensitivity to suffering, as if it were a second nature.

This is simply another way of describing virtue—in this case, the virtue of compassion. As such, it tends to be a permanent mode of being in the presence of suffering. It is not a transitory quality, experienced only on particular occasions or just for special persons. Rather, it has embedded itself in a person, endowing him or her with a permanent trait. This is no small accomplishment, since suffering, in the normal course of events, is not programmed to generate this kind of attitude. There are some sufferers who are the worse for what they undergo, not only physically, but also emotionally and attitudinally. They become embittered, angry, resentful people. This is understandable, since suffering is an evil, and seems an unlikely source for experiencing goodness on the part of those enveloped by it.

A pertinent scriptural example of compassion is the Good Samaritan parable. (Lk 10.29-37). However, as this story presents the man receiving the compassion of the Samaritan, it is unclear whether he reciprocated a similar love to him, so that a mutuality of love came to be experienced between them. Not even in the concluding scene, when the Samaritan, on his return journey, stopped at the inn again, to pay whatever further expenses were incurred by the innkeeper on behalf of the injured man, is the response of the victim indicated. Nonetheless, this would be a likely scenario.

A clearer biblical example of compassion is found in Mary standing at the foot of Jesus' cross. There she has come to be known as the Sorrowful Virgin or the Sorrowful Mother. We come to understand from this scene of Jesus' suffering that the love prevailing between her and her dying Son was truly mutual, and, though it preexisted this awful moment on Calvary, nonetheless reached a new level of intensity as she underwent her own intense suffering in conjunction with His own. Furthermore, tradition interprets this compassionate love of hers to extend, not only to her Son, but to all those included down the ages in Jesus' dying words to her and the disciple, John: "Woman, behold your son...Behold your mother". (Jn 19.26-27) As fellow-sufferers, each of them has been caught up in this far-reaching extension of compassion.

And, not least, of course, is the compassion of Jesus Christ Himself, which He displayed for others amid His own sufferings. For we have come to understand that He died on the cross for our sins and shared the sufferings we endured as a consequence. For the prophet Isaiah foretold: "Yet it was our infirmities that he bore, our sufferings that he endured...But he was pierced for our offenses, crushed for our sins,..." (53.4-5) He put Himself in a position where it could truly be said of Him that He entered into our share of humanity, experiencing everything that we do, even suffering and death, so that nothing human would remain foreign to Him, as Terentius says (pg. 23). He too embodied compassion, illustrating His own saying: "No one has greater love than this, to lay down one's life for one's friends." (Jn 15.13) To suffer for others in their need develops a bonding that is friendship. This kind of friendship is just another way of speaking about compassionate love. People bound together in suffering form a special kind of friendship extolled by Jesus, and compassion is the name for it.

When the zealot Saul was struck down on his way to Damascus, in search of Christians, he heard a voice asking: "Saul, Saul, why are you persecuting me?" (Acts 9.4) As we recall, in the course of the exchange that occurred, Saul came to understand who this ME was: it was the Christian community, whom he was seeking out to persecute. The risen Christ had so identified Himself with these suffering people that He and they were one person (the "me") undergoing the persecution Saul was inflicting. Compassion was still at work in the heart of the risen Christ, now beyond the trauma of suffering, despite still bearing wounds in His Hands, feet and side. (Jn 20.20) Yet He was so bonded with the Christian sufferers of a later time that they and He became one person in the cauldron of their suffering. Saul-become-Paul learned this well, as, in his later years as a Christian, he described the body of Christ in terms of each of us, its members. (1 Cor 12.12-31)

This same identity, based on similar experiences of suffering, is at work in the account of Mt. 25, as the King responds to the queries of those coming before Him, as to how they had, or had not, ministered to Him in His need, of water, food, shelter, clothing, visits, etc. Here again we note the bonding that compassion effected between the King and all those suffering in various ways. When they voiced their perplexed questions as to when their ministrations or omissions in the King's regard occurred, He responded in terms of His compassionate identity with each and every person undergoing those sufferings. So, even, and especially, at the end of time, the presence or absence of compassion will become the criterion of acceptance into or rejection from the kingdom of God.

Chapter 10

The Kingdom

Mt 25 addresses the finality awaiting us all. There is a King involved in this scene, together with a Kingdom awaiting our entrance. This too entails an experience, but, as a final one, it is of a very special kind, even though it centers around compassion, which we just considered, as the criterion determining whether we do or don't gain entry into this Kingdom.

From the early descriptions of our makeup (described as our perspectives and inclinations, which acquire further focus by way of fundamental option and vocation), through a varied set of experiences involving persons, especially God, church, culture, conscience, sin and suffering, and compassion, we now come to consider the finality before us. Though it will certainly be an experience, it will differ significantly from the ones just mentioned. It will indeed entail relationships, as do all experiences, but this final one will no longer be subject to our further agency. At this point, they enter into another dimension of relationship bringing us before Someone else Who will evaluate their goodness or evil.

Our entire life, prior to this moment, has been moving toward this encounter. We have been living in the forward mode. The future is ineradicably part of the perspective through which we have been looking, and our inclinations have been leaning toward it whether we recognized this or not. But, the moment comes when the future becomes present, and we find that the present is totally given over to looking back. At this juncture we will note again that, while hindsight continues to be keener than foresight, it is ultimately foresight, and the finality it leans toward, that will have proven to be determinative of our standing before the King. That will be a pleasant surprise if it can be shown that any past oversight, now clear by hindsight, has been insufficient to indict our foresight in providing quality moral agency. For, as the King makes clear in Mt 25, all of us will have failed to note His presence in our past experience, and this will have impaired the quality of conduct, for some of us, while, for others of us, it will thankfully not have condemned our behavior.

Prospects of this finality awaiting us should induce us to face it early on: the sooner, the better. We must recognize the rootage of the future in the present. This requires a special enhancement of our perspective that faith provides, adding penetration, breadth and far-sightedness to our outlook. Faith silhouettes the Kingdom's presence among us. It does this by inserting into our lives alertness to the prominence that Jesus assigned the Kingdom in His preaching and teaching ministry. This was not an incidental element of His message. It constituted its very heart.

This capacity to see the Kingdom looming before us is not ours to achieve; it is a gift from God. Once endowed with faith, of course, it is then up to us to nourish and augment it, and this takes place most readily within the setting provided by the church. The church is a harbinger of the kingdom, not identical with it, but the best symbol of it we find in this life. By presenting the scriptures and providing the sacraments, she makes available to us ingredients for growth in faith that few of us could achieve, by dint of our own resources, apart from the church. Our own spiritual pursuits, if taken in isolation from the institutional church, too lightly regard the incarnational mode of the Kingdom, prefigured in the church, given the importance the King places on such concrete matters as food, water, housing, clothing, etc.

In addition to the faith that enhances our perspectives and viewpoints, there is hope, and its potential for enriching our inclinations. It is comforting to recognize that, from early on, there were forces for good grappling to influence our inclinations, in opposition to the lures of evil, and that they first crystallized at the time of a fundamental option that helped our earlier inclinations to morph into a stance toward rather than away from, God. Corroborating energy became available in the

first indications of vocation or calling from God, which likewise per-
colated amid our inclinations. These incipient overtures benefit from
the nurturing and cultivation provided by hope, another gift of God,
provided to strengthen these inner movements coming to fruition in
the Kingdom of God.

Hope illustrates the biblical observation: "Whether a tree falls to the
south or to the north, wherever it falls, there shall it lie".(Eccl 11.3)
This kind of proclivity occurs in the setting of Mt 25, when what had
for so long been leaning toward the future now finally settles into place.
There is no longer a future to lean toward, but only the final moment
into which to fall. The lure of the Kingdom imparts hope to prompt
our inclinations, plans and strivings. As it does so, hope weeds out and
adjusts our tendencies, so that they lean in such a way as to fall toward
the kingdom.

The Kingdom fully blooms at the judgment seat of the King when He
reinterprets what all our experiences in this life have meant. This rein-
terpretation may conflict with our own understanding of where we are
coming from, in view of the question we all ask of the King: "when did
we see you.....?" We stand there, having accumulated experiences with
many persons, (not the least of whom is God), with the church (our
tutor on properly engaging one another, and especially God through
prayer and sacrament), with our culture, in all its many forms (the po-
litical, the economic, the educational, the professional, the organiza-
tional), with our own conscience, with the problems encountered in
life (especially sin, suffering and death) and with compassionate love for
the suffering.

Over a long life, these experiences accumulate into significance. Their
final assessment comes at the end, as finality, which has shadowed
everything along the way, at long last preempts everything else. Then
we will learn how the King evaluates them as He addresses us at the last
judgment. Our sacramental practices, our cultural achievements or failures, our conscience acuity, our handling of multiple negative experiences—all these will be noted by the King, but His focus will be on
compassion: for the sick, the homeless, the hungry, the thirsty, the im-
prisoned. While His evaluation will cover all the experiences of even a
long life trajectory, His attention will primarily focus on compassion.
While faith enlightens our perspective, and hope energizes our inclinations, compassionate love ennobles our experience.

As the Kingdom at last emerges into full presence, it comes accompanied by a lens through which to see our entire life, providing a focus that highlights what heretofore had not been so apparent. The future has this wonderful capacity to reinterpret the past, somewhat qualifying the conventional wisdom that hindsight is always better than foresight. In this case, the past is enhanced by the future so as to provide a sense of the present as each of us stands before the King. The value of appreciative inquiry will become evident, as we review, with the King's help, situations that have strewn our life path, and now see in them the opportunities that were available to us. At this point of end-time, our encounters with problems and negative experiences listed by the king (hunger, thirst, nakedness, imprisonment, illness) for which we sought no solution become part of a misspent past, that we can no longer change into opportunities by extending compassion to those in need.

The prospect of finality, understood in these terms, would help moral theology to appreciate the import of the invocation in the Lord's Prayer: "...Thy kingdom come..." Taking our stand before this better world to come is a powerful impetus for bettering the world we currently inhabit, on the conviction that good will ultimately prevail. If that be so, why engage in evil now? Commitment to the good life now is an early initiation of the goodness that will prevail in the life to come. Those who dismiss as irrelevant for the present what is to transpire in the future curtail the full impact of finality for bettering the present. The patina of the future adds luster to the present. The good takes on added promise in view of the better and the best that lies ahead. This proposal to strive for what is best may sound unsavory and self-centered, cheapening the pursuit of the good into a form of selfishness that co-opts it. But the promise latent in it recalls the role of promise throughout the history of the Hebrew people. (Dt 6.3, Jos 21.45, Mt 10.42, Acts 7.17) For they survived as a cohesive people to achieve their God-given role in history on the basis of cleaving to God's promises, constantly renewed, that empowered them toward their mission of bringing forth the Messiah into the world.

The future will finally help us adequately appreciate the dimensions of goodness in which we have engaged. Correspondingly, downplaying the future dulls our sense of evil and sin. When we pray, in The Lord's Prayer, "...Thy kingdom come...", we are invoking the moral impact of the future on our present life, since it comes in conjunction with: "...Thy will be done..." The future enhances both the good and the evil in our present experiences, constituting value-added quality to the good we do or enhancement to the evil we perform, should we fail to take the future into our regard. This comes home to roost in Mt 25 as the King, from the vantage point of the future-become-present, interprets the true dimensions of what we have been about in our lives.

The meaning of what we do or fail to do is the crucial issue that finality brings to a head. A sense of finality throws the significance of our current conduct into the condition of being penultimate, that is to say, the next to last. This does two things for appreciating our behavior: first, it links it to the truly ultimate and so allows what is final to bear upon the present; but, second, it indicates that our present moral agency is not yet the final determinant of our action, because that remains in the future. This corresponds to the way promise operates in our lives; it first brings to bear a future, completed, status upon a present, incomplete situation. At the same time, promise makes evident that what is at hand is incomplete, and awaits later fulfillment. While we have something to say and do regarding the penultimate or the promised, we have nothing to say or do regarding the ultimate upon its arrival, or regarding the promise fulfilled, because each of these lies beyond our control. This life, then, is but prelude to the final scenario. Eschatology is a term used to designate last or final things. The anticipation of the future in the present life constitutes a version of realized eschatology. So important is the influence of finality upon our life that we have multiple ways of appreciating its significance for us.

In its tradition, moral theology has incorporated the value of appreciating human performance in terms of finality. It has done this by employing the Latin terms *finis operis* and *finis operantis* as a way of assigning morality to our actions. These terms each incorporate a sensitivity to the end, or to finality, in explaining human agency. *Finis operis* focuses on an action in terms of its inner meaning, apart from any other meanings possibly accruing to it, as add-ons, from other sources, such as the agent him or herself.

There is something innate to every action that makes it what it is, and the moral agent, for instance, is not free to disregard or replace it. Giving money to a street person already has meaning in itself, apart from the variety of reasons we might have (the *finis operantis*) for doing so. This simply recognizes that we cannot reconstitute or restructure a deed by giving it a new purpose of our choosing. We must honor the meaning that is there, substantially from the finality built into it, though we are free to add further meanings to the meaning already there. We can do things for our own purposes. But each action has its own finality, and we do not have the ability to change or adjust it, even though we frequently try to argue that we performed a certain action for a finality we imposed on it, as a replacement for the purpose already inherent in it. However, it is interesting to note that there are finalities built into moral agency that only faith can discern, and we see them operative in Mt 25 as the King describes the fuller dimensions of what we do or fail to do.

In fact, the bible proves instructive in alerting us to dimensions accruing to our human agency from a faith vantage point that reflect a finality influence entering into the substance of an action. The brief moment of illumination, in the Transfiguration of Jesus on Mt. Tabor, illustrates the enlightenment of Peter, James and John about the Person they were following: Jesus.(Mt 17.1-13) The Transfiguration featured figures from the past (Moses and Elijah) appearing with Jesus, suggesting the compenetration of past, present and future (in terms of the glory enveloping them) into this fleeting moment. This shows that the meaning of Jesus was more complex than meets the eye. He embodies a richness whose fullness the three apostles had not yet fully understood.

And the scenes describing the risen Jesus' appearances to His followers address some questions about the final age, such as the meaning of the human body. What we currently know about the body awaits an amplification in the future when this body rises from the dead, possibly approximating the body of the risen Jesus, fully human to all intents and purposes, yet displaying capacities amplifying its meaning, such as the capacity to compenetrate other substances such as walls and closed doors, together with the ability for instantaneous and unforeseen appearances, as in the case of the apostles in the upper room in Jerusalem, or the disciples on their way to Emmaus, and the apostles fishing in the Sea of Tiberias, (Lk 24.13-49, Jn 21.1, ff.). These are graphic depictions of the impact that the finality presented in the Resurrection has upon the meaning of what we think we know so well: the human body.

These examples suggest that finality is not an incidental add-on, like icing on the cake. It's a constituent element in the meaning of things, including our behavior. Short of it, our actions are not finished; they are not yet what they seem to be. This is suggested by the descriptive term, "the way", (Acts 9.2, 19, 9) which was one of the early titles given to the Christian community: "followers of the way". This term aptly describes the reality, and the mindset, that should be ours. They, and we, were and are "on the way" to a destination, which will bring completion to our lives. We have here no final resting place. Our evaluation and measurement, the calculation of who we are, what we stand for and what we have accomplished, awaits a final tally in the time to come. We can't finally say, nor can others say, of us, who we are or what we have done or failed to do until finality arrives. We might take our cue in this from the thief whom Jesus addressed on the cross, since it was only at the end that he underwent the conversion that made him the person he finally became. (Lk 23.39-43) We could never say we knew the man, if we missed his final moment on earth. It is this kind of reasoning that opposes the death penalty, which curtails the life span of a criminal—time that might have brought a finality to his life comparable to that of the thief at Jesus' side, providing him that needed moment to change his fundamental option and thereby reconstitute his moral standing before God, becoming a new and different person in the process.

Over the years the church has been criticized for coddling deathbed converts. Perhaps some of this criticism has been deserved. But, mindful of the prominence of compassion in the final assessments awaiting us all before the judgment seat of the King, we would certainly want to be a candidate for the compassion of a last minute reprieve at the end, should final failure undo our otherwise stellar track record. (Ez 18.21-29)

Final perseverance in the terms that St. Paul has provided ("I have competed well; I have finished the race; I have kept the faith", 2 Tm 4.7) is ultimately gift, not personal accomplishment. Church tradition has encouraged praying for what she calls the gift of final perseverance. We do not earn it. We simply compete for it. We are much better advised, then, as we approach that judgment seat, to set aside the memory of our accomplishments ("I thank God that I am not like the rest of humanity...or even like this tax collector..." Lk 18.11), and to scoot over next to the publican, in the rear of the synagogue, and murmur ("Be merciful to me a sinner", 13).

And, in the meanwhile, we do well to invest in a GPS (Global Positioning System) that points us in the right direction, toward our finality. Such a system seems to have been in place on behalf of the Wise Men, in the form of a star guiding them to the place in Bethlehem where the child Jesus was to be found, with His mother and father. (Mt 2.1-12) It certainly "made their day" (10). Just as it brought closure to their journey, so can our sense of the end put us in touch with what will matter when we terminate our way through life and, like the Kings, take our place before another King, hopefully on his right. (Mt 25.33)

About the Author

The author has been a Catholic priest for almost 55 years. A native of Detroit, born of Kentucky-bred parents during the Great Depression, he left for the seminary at a very young age, while World War II was at its height, part of a large class of like-minded youth. Along the way, many of them departed for other pursuits in life, some of whom were to fight in the Korean conflict. Following ordination, he pursued further studies in Rome, and, before returning to the States, had the opportunity to sit in on moral theology courses taught by a young Bernard Haring, just arrived in Rome from Germany, and already well known for his groundbreaking work on *The Law of Christ*. Back in the States, he was soon caught up in the project of starting a new kind of seminary program at Catholic Theological Union in Chicago (CTU). After several years of teaching there, he left the academic field and became involved in the administration of the religious community to which he belonged (the Passionists), where he has spent the remainder of his life. This involvement brought him to every continent of the world, and considerably enriched his experience of life. Throughout this period of time he maintained his interest in moral theology, and managed to do some writing in the field. He has had a continuing relationship with CTU over the years, and currently sits on its board of trustees. Chicago has been his home for approximately half his life.

About the Book

During his teaching years, the author taught a variety of courses in moral theology (Christian Ethics). Many of these addressed specific areas of human agency: sexuality, marriage, business, technology, medicine, violence. Then it struck him one day that he was teaching about areas of conduct and behavior in most of which he had no personal or hands-on experience.

So his interest shifted to the basic foundations of moral theology where he, along with the rest of the human race, did have some expertise: what it means to be human. And, in addition, he pursued, together with many others in the field, what it means to act in a Christian/Catholic way, in any and all pursuits of life.

This book is a distillation of those areas of moral theology that address what all of us, or at least some of us, have in common: what it means to lead a decent human life, in a Christian way.

There are so many areas of specialization in our lives today that we can't communicate adequately with those who do not share our particular set of interests or concerns. We are separated from one another in significant areas of our lives. But we do have this in common: a desire to be good persons, acceptable and understandable to one another in the way we think and behave. On this basis we can live together, communicate intelligibly and cooperate with each other. We come to identify the values we share in common, and the rationale behind what we do or don't do.

Stealing Home is the title of this small book. It is obviously borrowed from baseball. It suggests that we want to win the game of life by gaining home—heaven, in the language familiar to many of us. The base pads leading to home plate are laid out here on the field of life before us.

Table of Contents

Dedication

To the memory of that generation of moral theologians/Christian ethicists who brokered the linkage between the fore and aft of the Second Vatican Council, especially Bernard Haring and his early *The Law of Christ*. The ongoing concern about continuity/discontinuity in moral theology reflects the early guideline proposed at the onset of the council: *ressourcement/aggiornamento*. The chrysalis process is still underway: the butterfly from the caterpillar.

Acknowledgment

Irene Horst devoted time and energy to the proof-reading of this book in its early stages. Lissa Rommel was always at hand to advise and instruct about the intricacies of the computer in its production. Some of my students from yesteryear periodically reminded me of the help they derived from the presentation found here, especially Richard Thomson, C.P. And Frederick Sucher, C.P., provided the assurance that the material in this small book conformed to the traditional corpus of moral doctrine sanctioned by the (Catholic) church.

Introduction

Variety is regarded as the spice of life. It characterizes the presentations of moral theology/Christian ethics the past fifty years, as it has other areas of theology. There is an increasing number of studies exploring ethical issues in contemporary life, presented by scholars who have devoted extensive time and effort to comprehending the field of specialization that interests them. Such efforts contribute greatly to the improvement of this discipline.

But, as in other areas of specialization, problems develop with knowing more and more about less and less. These were first noted in the medical field, where the term "specialist" became common in distinguishing those medical personnel who focused their attention on particular health issues, from others, who came to be called general practitioners, because their concern was the overall condition of their patients. Usually, these two medical types collaborate with one another.

This book falls in the latter category of concentration: the generalist. In doing so, it displays an interest in the combination of factors leading to a moral person. It takes its place alongside similar developments underway in moral theology, such as virtue ethics. Referring again to the medical field, divergences are also found in a generalist approach to health, such as the field of osteopathy, which differs in its understanding of what contributes to the overall health of persons, from the more common approach found in medical treatment.

The reader, then, of this small book is approaching a generalist, whose focus is more on the total or complete person, rather than on a focused area of concern, such as issues involving ecology, nuclear war, immigration, food supply, the educational system, the banking system, ethics in government, over-population, globalization, etc., most of which are social concerns more than personal ones. Nonetheless, the two are intertwined, since it is unlikely that a person can pursue his or her own individual welfare (moral/spiritual) without attending to problems affecting society at large.

These reflections have been inspired by similar ones from authors such as John Dewey, *Human Nature and Conduct*, Thomas Deman, *Aux Origenes de la Theologie Moral*, Joseph Sittler, *The Care of the Earth and Other University Sermons*, Herbert McCabe, *The Good Life: Ethics and the Pursuit of Happiness*, H.R. Niebuhr, *Christ and Culture*, Stanley Hauerwas, *Vision and Virtue*, and Paul Wadell, *Happiness and the Christian Moral Life*.

And, then, of course, there are the Scriptures. Replete with the teachings of Jesus, they are also a treasury of prayer, especially in the book of Psalms. When all is said and done, any success we enjoy in moving away from moral evil and sin in our life and toward a good life is the workings of prayer, invoking God to come to our assistance, and help our effort at stealing home.

Sebastian MacDonald, C.P.

10 media/book publishing industry contacts provided, including contact information:

The following are all journals featuring book review sections in each issue:

Editor, Horizons, St. Mary's Hall, Villanova University, 800 Lancaster Ave., Villanova PA 19085

Irish Theological Quarterly, Pontifical University, St. Patrick's College, Maynooth, Co. Kildare, Ireland

New Blackfriars, Review Editors, Viviana Boland & Gregory Peerson, Blackfriars, Oxford OX1, 3LY, UK

The Editors, New Theology Review, Catholic Theological Union, 5416 S. Cornell Ave., Chicago IL 60615

Rivista di teolgia morale, Centro Editoriale Dohoniano, Via Nosadella, 6 – 40123, Bologna, Italia

Studia Moralia, Editiones Academico Alfonsianae, Via Merulana, 31, 00185 Roma, Italia

Theological Studies Book Reviews, U. of San Francisco-Kalmanovitz 152, 2130 Fulton St., San Francisco CA 94117-1080

Theology, SPCK, 36 Causton St., London SWIP 4ST, UK

Gordon S. Mikoski, editor, Theology Today, P.O. Box 821, Princeton NJ 08542-0803

The Editors, Toronto Journal of Theology, Toronto School of Theology, 47 Queen's Park Crescent East, Toronto Ontario Canada M5S2C3